Tools of Thinking: Understanding the World through Experience and Reason
Part II

Professor James H. Hall

THE TEACHING COMPANY ®

PUBLISHED BY:

THE TEACHING COMPANY
4151 Lafayette Center Drive, Suite 100
Chantilly, Virginia 20151-1232
1-800-TEACH-12
Fax—703-378-3819
www.teach12.com

ISBN 1-59803-086-8

James H. Hall, Ph.D.
Thomas Professor of Philosophy, Emeritus, University of Richmond

Born in Weimar, Texas, in 1933, I spent my early childhood there and in New Orleans, Louisiana. Just before World War II, my family moved to Washington, D.C. I lived in that city and received my education from its public schools, museums, and newspapers, until I went off to college in Baltimore, Maryland, in the fall of 1951.

I knew *that* I wanted to teach by the time I graduated from high school, but I didn't know *what* I wanted to teach until much later. So I made a career of being a student for 12 more years (at Johns Hopkins University, Southeastern Theological Seminary, and the University of North Carolina at Chapel Hill), before trying to earn a living full time.

I had discovered my discipline by 1959, but it was 1965 before I found my school and my city. Each of the 40 years since then has confirmed my good fortune in joining the University of Richmond community and putting my roots down.

Teaching is my calling and first professional priority. I am especially gratified to have been declared "Outstanding Faculty Member of the Year" by both Omicron Delta Kappa and the Student Government of the University of Richmond at the end of my last year in the classroom. With 44 years at the blackboard, I have taught most of the standard undergraduate philosophy curriculum, including *Symbolic Logic*, *Moral Issues*, and *Philosophical Problems* to thousands of beginners and advanced courses and seminars on *Analytic Philosophy* (especially the works of Russell, Ayer, Wittgenstein, Ryle, and Austin), *Philosophy of Religion*, and *Epistemology* to hundreds of philosophy majors and minors. I have also pursued a number of issues beyond the boundaries of philosophy per se, in interdisciplinary courses as varied as *Science and Values*; *The Ideological Roots of the American Revolution*; and *Science, Pseudoscience and the Paranormal*. My research has produced an adult education series for The Teaching Company (*Philosophy of Religion*) and three published books (*Knowledge, Belief and Transcendence*; *Logic Problems*; and *Practically Profound*), with another in progress (*Taking the Dark Side Seriously*).

A life totally confined to the ivied tower would be truncated and precarious. My own is constantly expanded and kept in balance by ongoing involvements in church (Episcopal), politics (Democratic), and choral music (from Bach to Durafle, with just a dash of Ralph Vaughan Williams) and by travel (Wales or the Pacific northwest for preference) and a daily bout with the *New York Times* crossword. Many people outside of the academy have enriched my life by their work—Herblock and Harry Truman, John D. MacDonald and David Lodge, to name four—and others by their friendship and character—chief among them my wife, Myfanwy, and my sons, Christopher, Jonathan, and Trevor.

My complete track record, academic and otherwise, can be seen on the Web at: http://www.richmond.edu/~jhall/.

E-mail will always reach me at: jhall@richmond.edu.

Table of Contents

Tools of Thinking: Understanding the World through Experience and Reason
Part II

Tools of Thinking: Understanding the World through Experience and Reason

Scope:

Whenever we decide to do a little thinking, a variety of tools are available for the enterprise. Perhaps we will try to remember what we already know or believe (regardless of how we came by it). Perhaps we will try to deduce something from what we already know or believe. Perhaps we will engage in the give and take of dialectic. Perhaps we will try to identify patterns in what we already know or believe (and remember) that would allow us to generalize it or extrapolate from it to claims of broad (or even universal) scope. Perhaps we will give free rein to the flow of our ideas, allowing them to call one another before the mind's eye in some pattern of association. Perhaps we will turn to sense experience and experimentation to provide the raw materials for some belief or knowing. Perhaps we will invent a model, hypothesis, metaphor, or rule to try to hang all or part of what we believe or know together in some systematic way. Or perhaps we will engage in a vigorous round of hypothesis and counterexample. Whatever tools we use, it is likely that we will, at some point, appeal to "intuition" to back up the general enterprise or some particular foundational piece of it. Whatever tools we use, of course, will involve some risks.

The purpose of this course is to trace out in a semi-historical way how modern rational empiricism has arrived at its tool kit for thinking (a tool kit particularly well modeled by modern natural science but also employed in a wide variety of other, everyday, enterprises). We will look at some of the ideas of Plato, Aristotle, Descartes, Hume, and Newton, interspersed with some representative attention to the methods and limitations of classical syllogistic logic, modern sentential and predicate logic, and Mill's theory of induction. We will also note the necessity of making room for conceptual invention when setting up general principles to organize our thoughts and give close attention to the crucial roles of hypothesis construction and experimentation in the thinking of modern rational empiricists.

As we work through these matters, we will note the frequent occurrence of broadly skeptical ideas about the very possibility of thinking reliably. These include Plato's mistrust of appearances,

Descartes' mistrust of sense experience, Hume's mistrust of all general claims, the logical empiricists' mistrust of any claim that is untestable, and postmodern concerns about paradigms and paradigm shifts and the extent to which our thinking is controlled by the culture in which we find ourselves. The purpose of this course, however, is not the refutation of general or systematic skepticism. I have dealt with that in another work— see my *Practically Profound* (Lanham: Roman and Littlefield, 2005), Part I (Belief) and Part II (Knowledge). The present concern, rather, is to show how the various tools that we use in our thinking can lead us to generally reliable (not perfect) beliefs and useful (not certain) knowledge. Further, while any number of thinkers would add revelation and faith to the items set out in the first paragraph here, the purpose of this course does not include the systematic examination of such matters. (I have dealt with them in my Teaching Company course of 2003, *Philosophy of Religion*). The present concern, rather, is to explore the tools that are appropriate to more mundane matters, such as science, history, and navigating the everyday vicissitudes of life.

One thing will emerge from these reflections: There is no *one* tool for thinking. Experience by itself begets chaos in the absence of pattern recognition, memory, association, and some form of reasoning. Reason by itself is sterile absent some practically reliable bases from which to draw our inferences, explanations, and generalizations. Intuition by itself offers no decision procedure. Invention by itself is dangerously speculative. The magic is in the mix.

Because this course is a broad and rapid survey of vast and complex matters, it will not answer all (or even most) of the questions that will occur to you along the way about the mind, our sensory apparatus, belief, knowledge, reasoning, and logic, much less about mathematics, science, philosophy, ethics, and all the other great systematic ventures of the mind. It will, however, deal with some of the important ones and provide references to works where many of the others can be explored. It is a starting point, not a destination.

Lecture Thirteen
Proper Inferences Avoid Equivocation

Scope:

If we rely on experiences as evidence for our inferences and explanations, we must screen the ways in which we handle those that offer themselves so as to avoid making unwarranted presumptions about them and to avoid exploiting their ambiguity in various tempting ways. Otherwise, we may be guilty of fallacies of presumption and ambiguity in a variety of ways. Several representative types of such fallacies are explained in this lecture, and examples are provided. Examining them will help us avoid egregious errors in our thinking. Although thinking that commits such fallacies is common, it is always misleading.

Outline

I. If we rely on experiences (or anything else for that matter) as evidence for our inferences and explanations, we must screen the ways in which we handle them in order to avoid making unwarranted presumptions about them and equivocating over what they mean.

    A. These cautions are also prerequisites for useful inference drawing.

    B. When we presume, in one way or another, facts that are not in evidence, and when we play fast and loose with the meanings of our locutions, we are (once again) "not even in the ballpark, much less in the game."

II. Here are descriptions and examples of eight forms that such bad reasoning can take.

    A. *Petitio principii.* This fallacy amounts to inferring a conclusion from premises that are, in fact, indistinguishable from the conclusion itself. This fallacy is also called *circular reasoning* and *question begging*.

    Example: I know that God exists because the Bible says so. And I know that everything in the Bible is true because it is God's word and God wouldn't lie.

B. *Complex question.* This fallacy amounts to presuming without evidence that a certain state of affairs obtains, then shaping one's inquiry in terms of that presumption.

Example: The classic is "Have you stopped beating your wife?" but it is equally clear in "Don't you want to be a good boy and go to bed?"

C. *Equivocation.* This amounts to exploiting ambiguities of words. Some are simple plays on an everyday noun or adjective. Some exploit the subtleties of dispositional and episodic participles.

Examples: When mother asks, "Were you good at the party, Susie?" Susie responds, "Well, Miles said I was." When father asks, "Are you smoking [these days], Fred?" Fred responds, "No I'm not [right this moment]."

D. *Amphibole*. This fallacy amounts to exploiting ambiguities of syntax.

Example: A subway rider explains why he lit a cigar right next to the sign that said "No Smoking Allowed" by noting the two ways that sign can be read: "Smoking is forbidden" and "Refraining from smoking is permitted."

E. *Accent.* This fallacy amounts to exploiting ambiguities of emphasis, including selective data use.

Example: Story positioning in the media, headline writing, and small print on a box of Broccoli Rice Surprise show just what accent can do.

F. *Category mistake.* This fallacy amounts to exploiting ambiguities of classification. The term comes from Gilbert Ryle's *The Concept of Mind.*

Example: Not seeing the forest for all the trees, the parade for all the marchers, and the university for all the buildings and greens are all examples of confusing things and systems. "If we have minds, then where are they?" is a more telling case in point.

G. *Composition* and *division.* These fallacies amount to exploiting ambiguities between the properties of individuals and the properties of the sets that they compose.

Example: "Everyone in my gymnastics class is *tiny*. There's no one there over 80 pounds. I can't see why the instructor is complaining that the class is too big."

H. *False dilemma.* This fallacy amounts to exploiting ambiguities of complementarity.

Example: "Well, Ali was certainly no hero, so he must have been a coward."

Essential Reading:

Irving Copi, *Introduction to Logic*, Chapter 4, Sections 3 and 4 ("Fallacies of Presumption" and "Fallacies of Ambiguity"), pp. 156ff.

Recommended Reading:

W. Ward Fearnside, *Fallacy: The Counterfeit of Argument*.

Questions to Consider:

1. Why do you suppose that one must swear to tell the truth, the whole truth and nothing but the truth in court? Why isn't it enough just to swear not to lie?

2. Why do you suppose that when Clinton was asked, "Did you have sexual relations with XYZ?" he responded, "Are we talking Arkansas Code here?"

Lecture Thirteen
Proper Inferences Avoid Equivocation

When we rely on our experiences, or whatever else for that matter, as a basis for our inferences and our explanations, we need to be quite careful to screen them to be sure that we are not presuming they are not in evidence, to be sure that we are avoiding any kind of unwarranted presumption, and to be sure that we are avoiding any kind of equivocation. Being cautious about presumptions and equivocations is just as important as being cautious about relevance, which was the matter we talked about last time. Avoiding equivocation and avoiding unwarranted presumptions are prerequisites to good argument—just as relevance is a prerequisite to good arguments. When we do not pay attention to those matters, then, once again, we are "not even in the ball park, much less in the game itself."

There are a number of ways in which unwarranted presumptions and equivocation can creep into our arguments, and today I am going to innumerate a number of them, explain them, and give you examples of how they work. But let me underscore at the beginning that these are not examples of good arguments. These are examples of bad arguments, of things to avoid.

The first one that I want to talk about has been recognized and known long enough that it is known by the Latin name *Petitio principii*, meaning *begging the question*, or *arguing in circles*. This way of fallacious reasoning amounts to inferring a conclusion from a set of premises, when in fact the conclusion itself is so inseparably packed into the presumptions that you are making, that it is already there. Let me give you an example from a student I had in a class a number of years ago who told me that he had read an absolute knockdown proof of the existence of God. That was of interest to me because philosophy of religion is an area in which I have a great interest. So, I said, "Tell me, what is this absolute proof?" And he said, "Well it goes this way. I know that God exists because the Bible says that God exists, and I know that everything in the Bible is true because the Bible is God's word, and God wouldn't lie."

Maybe you get the feeling for packing your conclusion into your presumptions in such a way that they are inseparable. But a *question begging, circular reasoning*, or *petition*, as we often say, explanation or account can sound profound. If you go to the doctor with some itchy, irritated condition on your skin, and the doctor strokes his chin wisely and says that you have dermatitis, maybe you will feel illuminated and informed. But what the doctor has just told you is that you have this itchy condition of your skin, all irritated, *derma tutus*. It is irritated skin. To what can we can we attribute the soporific effect of opium? Why to its formative potency? Circularity can turn into bad jokes, but it is something that you want to avoid insofar as you can.

Now, a side bar. There is a sense in which every deductive argument is circular. If the conclusion that you are trying to establish deductively is not in the premises somewhere, then how could you argue your way from the premises to that conclusion? The problem with a question-begging argument is that the conclusion simply as such on its face is right there. It is not so much that the argument is circular, but that the circle is very small. It is tiny enough to make you dizzy.

Another classic fallacy of equivocation and improper presumption is called the fallacy of *complex question*. Complex question is what happens when you, as we say in court, presume facts that are not in evidence, and then let those presumptions color and shape your inquiry as to determine the type of outcome that is possible. The classic example of this is the question in court allegedly—"Have you stopped beating your wife?" Well that presumes that you were at one time and consequently needed to stop, and so on. It is equally present in the kind of technique we use to try to cajole our children. "Sonny, don't you want to be a good boy and go to bed?" Well, yes, Sonny wants to be a good boy, but Sonny does not want to go to bed, and it is not at all clear on the face of things what one has to do with the other.

Well, apart from complex questions and circularity, there is just plain and simple *equivocation*. I want to spend a little bit more time on that because this is really the dangerous one. Now, equivocation can happen in several different ways. The most obvious kind of equivocation is where we are equivocating directly over the multiple ambiguous meanings of a single term. And as all of us realize if we stop to think about it for a second, most of the nouns that we use in the English language have more than one use. They have more than one meaning. They are ambiguous and consequently they are ripe for equivocating, playing fast and loose between the different meanings in the terms.

There is a classic case of this that I will tell you briefly that goes back to Gary Trudeau's college years from a comic strip before he started drawing Doonesbury. The comic is one in which a young woman is going out on a date. The house-mother, or her mother, or whoever the woman is in the panel says to her, "Now, Susie, be good." The young woman goes with the young man, and there are a couple of panels in the comic strip where we simply see a car parked by the side of a lake, and there are brevets and squiggles to indicate the car is rocking on its wheels, and so on. Then, in the last panel, Susie's coming back into the house and hitching up her skirt with one hand and straightening herself out, and the lady says to her, "Susie, were you good?" Susie replies, "Well, Miles said I was." Susie knew perfectly well what her mother meant when she asked "Were you good?" Susie knew perfectly well what Miles meant when he said she was good. And Susie is equivocating between those two meanings of good in an attempt to deceive.

It can get more complicated than that. Equivocation is not always over two simple, straightforward meanings of the same term. It can even get into something as technical as the difference between an episodic interpretation of a term and a dispositional interpretation of the same term. I remember one time, much to my shame, my father called me when I was an undergraduate in college and asked me on the telephone, "Are you smoking?" Click, click, click, the wheels started to go around. Now, is he asking me this episodically or dispositionally? Terms he would not have even recognized. But I looked quickly. There was nothing burning in either hand. There was nothing hanging out of the side of my mouth, and so I answered episodically, "No, I'm not right now." But I'm sure what my father had in mind was if I was disposed to smoke from time to time; a true answer to which would have been, regrettably, yes. But taking advantage of the fact that there is a difference between episodes and dispositions, I equivocated in order to mislead.

Equivocation is even broader than that because the slipperiness of the meaning in a locution may be imbedded in the syntax rather than in the actual words that are used. There is a famous story—I do not know whether it is true or not. But there is a famous story of a man who sat down on a subway car in New York, or Boston, or some place where there are subways. That could even be Washington these days. He sat right under a sign that said, "No smoking allowed," and he took out a big cigar and lit it. Upon being confronted by the guard as to why he would do this right in the very presence of the sign, the man said, "Well, I appreciate the fact that the transit authority is so generous as to allow me to not smoke, but I thought I'd just go ahead and do something anyway." 'No smoking allowed,' and here is a 50-cent word for you: 'No smoking allowed' is an *amphibolous*. You can read it as saying, refraining from smoking is permitted, or you can read it as saying that smoking is prohibited. You could read it either way.

Accent is the playground of newspaper editors' headline writers. The meaning of a claim or the meaning of an argument can be bent and adjusted in terms of placement, in terms of emphasis, and consequently it can radically change the message that comes across. When I was a young man teaching at a school that I will not name, in a town that I will not name, there was a political campaign going on, and this was a long time ago. The political campaign of this particular instance was for the republican nomination for the presidency. And the two candidates who were vying for that republican nomination were Nelson Rockefeller and Barry Goldwater. The newspaper in the little town where I happened to be at the time was a passionate supporter of the Goldwater candidacy. On one particular occasion, as luck would have it, Mr. Rockefeller was delivering a major public policy address on the West Coast, but this was one of the important pieces of the platform on which he was running to seek the nomination.

And Goldwater, smart politician that he was, saw no need to compete head-to-head. This was Nelson's day, and so Goldwater took a day off. So we had a news day in which there was a major Rockefeller event but no Goldwater event. Ah, but the editors of that local newspaper were creative. They dug back in the files, finding a picture of Mr. Goldwater on a gurney with his sleeve rolled up and tubing attached to his arm. They ran this above the gatefold on the front page of the newspaper with the screamer headline, "Barry Gives Blood." Back on about page 82, somewhere between the obituaries and the horoscope, there was a small little story to the effect that Rockefeller delivered a political pot-boiler on the West Coast. Non-facts were not reported. Untruths were not mentioned.

But the impact that came across because of placement, because of emphasis, or because of what logicians call *accent*, was definitely tailored for a certain effect.

This can show up in other places too. I will never forget the day that I had a craving for broccoli. I really enjoy broccoli, and I was doing some shopping in the market, and I saw a package that was labeled *Broccoli Rice Surprise. Broccoli Rice Surprise*—I should have been more cautious. I thought that sounded really good. It had a beautiful picture on the front of the box with big broccoli florets and a little rice scattered around. I took it home. Ninety-seven percent of what was in the package was macaroni—that was the surprise. Rice was 3.9 percent, and maybe 0.1 percent of it was broccoli. There certainly was broccoli; there certainly was rice—and there certainly was an enormous surprise. But by placement, accent, picture, and emphasis, the seller was able to project an image that clenched the sale.

Now we go on to something a little more subtle. And this is philosophically quite important. There is something that philosophers call *category mistake*. The label goes back to a British philosopher named Gilbert Ryle who was in his prime in the mid-20th century. Category mistakes are situations where we mis-categorize a phenomenon. We put it in the wrong slot. We try to interpret it and understand it in terms of the wrong concepts, and consequently we wind up with chaos and confusion. Now, the notion of the category mistake is not an esoteric philosophical notion. It is built into clichés in the language. An example is when we talk about not being able to see the forest for the trees. "Somebody told me there was a forest around here somewhere, but where is it? All these trees are in the way, I can't see the forest."

Stop and think about that for a moment. A forest is a systemic notion. A forest is a particular way of having a lot of trees organized and put together in one place at one time. But the forest is not anything more than that arrangement of the trees in one place at one time. Ryle, in his deservedly famous book, *The Concept of Mind*, illustrated the notion of a category mistake with the story of a young man who came down to Oxford to examine the university and to decide whether or not he wanted to spend three or four years of his life at the university. As Ryle charmingly tells the story, the young man wanders through Oxford City up past Carfax and maybe all the way up to the top of Headington Hill and back down again to the center of town. There is New College, Maudlin, and the Baudley, and then there are examination schools. But he comes away perplexed and scratching his head because, he said, "I spent hours going back and forth, up and down every street in Oxford looking for the university, and I never found it." Well, a university is a systemic thing, or a university is a system. A university is composed of colleges, libraries, dormitories, commons buildings, and all the rest—organized and structured in a particular way. It is more than that because the structure that constitutes a university also incorporates a structure of people. It incorporates researchers, teachers, scholars, and students.

All of this has to be put together in a certain way, functioning in a certain way, before we have a university. And let me say, not meaning to be unkind at all, simply a rude truth; one does not necessarily find a university every time one sees on the map the label, University of X. The structure may not be there. Some of the constituent parts may be missing. They may not be strung together in the right kind of way to generate that unique and glorious system phenomenon of the university.

I am leaning on this one because this one is important, and I am going to lean on it for just one more example—Ryle's point, the mind. Is the mind one more piece of the organism? Does it have a specific location? Do we find it perhaps hidden somewhere just behind the pineal gland? Or, as Ryle argues, is the mind a system, a particular way of organizing and putting together an organic whole that functions in particular useful and creative ways? If so, then there is a whole history of philosophical inquiry into the location of the mind, and the characteristics of the mind, and whether or not the mind and the body are made out of different kinds of stuff as Ryle saw it, dreadfully wrong-headed.

So, as he writes about the concept of mind in that watershed book, he is arguing that an organism can be organized in such a way that it has mental capacities and functions. An organism could be organized in such a way that it does not have mental capacities and functions, and the difference between those two organisms would not be the presence or the absence of a part or a piece. It would be the presence or absence of a particular dynamic structure.

Now, my point today is not to try to argue that Ryle is right or wrong about his analysis of the mental. I do underscore it because it is a very important chapter in the history of philosophy of mind. We have said a bit earlier on about Descartes, and we will be seeing some more later about Descartes. So when the occasion arises for you to read Descartes, you might read a little Ryle alongside of it. My point, though, is that this is one of the most dangerous kinds of presumptions and equivocations that can occur—an equivocation between what I am going to call *substance terms* and *system terms*, or *substance terms* and *process terms*. We have a tendency, and it goes back, I think, and again we have mentioned Plato and Aristotle, it goes back to Plato's notion that we differentiate things in terms of the substances from which they are made. And so when we see differences between X, Y, and Z, there is a natural tradition-driven impulse to go looking for the substantial difference that is behind the functional difference.

But almost as honorable and ancient as that Platonic substantial analysis is the Aristotelian functional analysis. And what Ryle was doing in the 20th century was bringing us back in focus on the notion that things can differ, not only in terms of what they are made of, but they can differ in terms of how they are put together.

There is one more point on this, and then we will move on. Think about the number of different ways in which you can take the same substantial material and fashion it into differently functioning systems. Think of silicon, the primary ingredient of sand—and sand, in turn, is a primary ingredient of concrete. But silicon is also a primary ingredient of integrated circuit chips, which are a primary ingredient of computers. Substantially, the bulk of what is involved in a lump of concrete, and the bulk of what is involved in an integrated computer circuit, is the same. The structure, however, is radically different, and, consequently, the function is radically different. And if we make the mistake of equivocating between substance and function, we can lead ourselves on a merry chase into unanswerable metaphysical questions.

Composition and division are enough like a kind of fallacy we talked about last time, the fallacy of *hasty generalization* and *accident*. They are enough like those that they can be confusing, so I want to be careful with them. You will remember hasty generalization is when you go from the characteristics of a limited number and take a great flying leap to the conclusion that everything has those characteristics. Accident is just the reverse of that. When you see that the members of a group predominantly have these characteristics then you take a flying leap to the conclusion that a particular member of the group must have that characteristic just like the rest of them do.

Composition and division are different, although they look a little bit like that. In composition and division, what we are doing is equivocating between the properties of sets themselves and the properties of the individuals or members that make up those sets. Stop and think about it for a moment. You can readily see that a set could have certain characteristics or properties, and that the individuals that make up a set could also have certain characteristics and properties, and they are not the same thing at all. Now this might not be confusing if it were not for the fact that we sometimes use the same words to talk about properties of individuals that we use to talk about properties of sets.

You can make a bad joke out of this. I visualize a child who is taking gymnastics class, and I visualize the instructor of the gymnastics class complaining to the person who is running the school that the class is just too big. The child is scratching her head and wondering how that could be the case because there is not a single individual in the class who weighs over 85 pounds. But, of course, you can have a big class of little people—or, for that matter, you could have a little class of big people. You know, one of the things that we college professors worry about is class size, and we like to argue, at any rate, that a class that is limited in its size makes for better teaching. Well, could I legitimately complain if I went in to teach a logic class one day, and there were four students in the class, but all of them were sumo-wrestlers weighing in at 500 pounds a piece? Boy, what a large class that would be!

So, we have to be careful. We have to be very careful about what properties belong to the group, what properties belong to the members of the group, and not equivocate back and forth between them. It is perfectly legitimate for the intercollegiate athletic governing bodies—they have long since done it, to limit the size of a football team in terms of the number of people that are allowed to be on the team. But it would be the worst kind of folly to lodge some complaint with the governing body of your athletic league, that such and such a school was violating the rules right and left because, look at the tackles and linebackers that they have on their team. They all weigh in at about 300 pounds a piece.

Lastly, *false dilemma* will be our last one for today. False dilemma happens when we trap ourselves into thinking improperly, that the options or alternatives in a given situation are more limited than they are. And so we say we are trapped—we have a dilemma here, we have to do this, or we have to do that, and those are all the options that there are. When, in fact, there are other options.

Classic examples of false dilemma trade on a misunderstanding of the relationship of complementarity that we have talked about before. You will remember that every class has its complement. The complement of a class is everything else. So if something is not a member of the class P, it is going to be a member of the class non-P. But if you make the mistake of thinking that opposite or disagreeing terms are complementary, you might then wrongfully infer that simply because someone was not a hero, they must be a coward, going back to the example that I used earlier on. But, of course, heroes and cowards are not complementary classes at all. There are hundreds of other alternative categories into which people can be sorted out.

Lecture Fourteen
Induction Is Slippery but Unavoidable

Scope:

Generalizing over particulars is a problematic way to establish universal claims. The first "problem of induction" is the alleged circularity of all such reasoning. Whether that problem can be effectively solved or is simply shelved, other issues remain about the methods to use to reach general truths, about the probabilistic limitations of such methods, and about the reliability of the bases of our inferences. After making a pragmatic assumption about the regularity of nature, we will look at John Stuart Mill's classic analysis of the inductive methods of *agreement, difference, residues,* and *concomitant variation.* These are illustrated with examples to help us understand what induction can do and its limitations. Then, after a brief look (in Lecture Fifteen) at a simplified account of Newton's "hypothesis-free" explanations, the stage will be set for a discussion (in Lecture Sixteen) of how explanatory hypotheses are constructed and used in contemporary science.

Outline

I. Even if questions of relevance, ambiguity, and presumption have been satisfactorily taken care of, generalizing over particulars is a problematic way to establish universal claims.

    A. The first problem of induction is basic.

        1. Predicting that unobserved or future events will be like the events that are or have been observed assumes the uniformity of nature.

        2. But if the only reason to think that nature will remain uniform is that it has done so thus far, then this assumption is clearly circular or question begging, as Hume notes.

        3. Are there any other reasons to think that nature is uniform? An appeal to natural law is equally circular, appeals to divine constancy or the immutability of the Forms lack any experiential grounds, and an appeal to intuition or insight is radically subjective.

4. If we cannot effectively "prove" induction, we can bite the bullet and beg the question. There is little practical advantage to be gained by *not* presuming the uniformity of nature.

B. Even if we simply shelve this problem, however, other issues remain about the methods to use to reach general truths, about the probabilistic limitations of such methods, and about the bases of our inferences.

   1. Something more than simple enumeration of similarities is called for because this takes no notice of disconfirming instances and, hence, provides no effective test for any putative natural law.

   2. Inductive inferences are probabilistic, at best. They don't provide closure:

      a. They "affirm the consequent" (if P then Q; Q, therefore P).

      b. They presume that surprises will not occur in nature.

      c. They may, in any instance, overlook alternative accounts.

   3. Our inferences are no stronger than their bases. Consequently, all of the difficulties with the reliability of experience, as well as with the reliability of our recall and pattern recognition, come into play.

II. John Stuart Mill provides a useful analysis of inductive methods in *A System of Logic*, identifying the techniques of agreement, difference, residues, and concomitant variation.

   A. *Mill's method of agreement*: "If two or more instances of the phenomenon under investigation have only one circumstance in common, the circumstance in which alone all the instances agree is the cause (or effect) of the given phenomenon."

   Example: Looking for an itinerant Typhoid Mary.

   B. *Mill's method of difference*: "If an instance in which the phenomenon under investigation occurs and an instance in which it does not occur have every circumstance in common, save one, that one occurring only in the former, the circumstance in which alone the two instances differ is the effect, or the cause, or an indispensable part of the cause of the phenomenon."

   Example: Autopsies, hand washing, and childbed fever.

C. Mill's methods of agreement and difference can be used together.

   Example: Using control groups and switchover testing for pharmaceuticals.

D. *Mill's method of residues*: "Subtract from any phenomenon such part as is known by previous inductions to be the effect of certain antecedents, and the residue of the phenomenon is the effect of the remaining antecedents."

   Example: Isolating the effect of video gaming on eye-hand coordination.

E. *Mill's method of concomitant variation*: "Whatever phenomenon varies in any manner whenever another phenomenon varies in some particular manner is either a cause of that phenomenon or is connected with it through some fact of causation."

   Example: Carefully tracking behaviors of ADD children when on and off their meds.

III. These methods and examples help us understand what induction can and cannot do.

   A. Induction can suggest hypotheses to "try on for size" and usefully *test* the ones we come up with.

   B. Induction can't *prove* a hypothesis.

   1. Induction yields only probability.

   2. Induction can operate in ignorance of crucial variables.

   3. Induction can't rule out alternative hypotheses that haven't been thought of yet.

IV. After a brief look (in Lecture Fifteen) at a simplified account of Newton's "hypothesis-free" explanations, the stage will be set for a discussion (in Lecture Sixteen) of how explanatory hypotheses are constructed and used in contemporary science.

Essential Reading:

Irving Copi, *Introduction to Logic*, Chapter 12, Part 2, "Mill's Methods," pp. 455ff.

Recommended Reading:

Paul De Kruif, *Microbe Hunters*.

Questions to Consider:

1. What is wrong with Mark Twain's famous induction that his lack of dental problems is the result of his predilection for rye whiskey?

2. What is wrong with Erich Von Daniken's inference (in *Chariots of the Gods*) that some artifacts that he observed in the Yucatan jungle were litter from space-alien visitations?

Lecture Fourteen
Induction Is Slippery but Unavoidable

Once we are reasonably sure that the evidence that we are going to be using is relevant to the issue that we are trying to deal with, and once we can reasonably be sure that we have avoided equivocation and have avoided unwarranted presumptions along the way, we then move forward to reason. And one of the most common patterns that we use is to generalize from particular individual experiences that we have had, to reach more encompassing, more blanket-covering, statements—maybe even covering law for situations of that kind. But even if questions of relevance, ambiguity, and presumption have been satisfactorily taken care of, there are still problems. While generalizing over particulars is probably the most common and most simple kind of inductive inference that we carry out, it can be severely problematic at many levels.

There is a story told of a scientist who was trying to figure out why he kept waking up in the morning with a terrible headache. And he reasoned, well, saying, "Monday night I drank brandy and soda and woke up Tuesday morning with a headache. Tuesday night I drank scotch and soda and woke up Wednesday morning with a headache. Wednesday night I drank bourbon and soda and woke up Thursday morning with a headache. I've just got to stop drinking soda." Yes, there are problems of identifying the key variables. There are a lot of problems, as we shall see.

I want to start with a problem today, however, that is more generic than that. Rock-bottom basic. It is called the "problem of induction." Here is what it amounts to: predicting that unobserved states of affairs or future events are going to be essentially like states of affairs that we have observed or events that are in the past presumes that nature itself is regular. It presumes what is called the "uniformity of nature." If nature were not uniform then there would be no way to move from what we have observed to some prediction about what has not yet been observed. The uniformity or regularity of nature is absolutely essential for that kind of inference to move forward. But what kind of reason do we have to think that nature is uniform? Well, it has always been so far—but of course, that is the very issue at stake. To think that nature is going to remain uniform because it has been uniform is just one more instance of predicting the unobserved on the assumption that—the unjustified assumption that—it's going to be essentially like those things that we have already observed.

Well, then, are there any reasons that we might have other than it has always worked so far, to induce? Well, we might try appealing to Natural Laws. But, believe me, to appeal to Natural Laws is nothing more than a fancy way of appealing to the uniformity of nature. The very notion that there are Natural Laws is one way of flushing out the idea that nature itself is uniform or regular. Similarly for appeals to divine constancy, or if we are feeling terribly platonic on a given occasion, appealing to the immutability of the forms, these are all fancier ways of talking about the same presumption—that the future will be like the past, and that what we have not yet seen will be like what we have seen.

Well, if we cannot effectively "prove" that nature is uniform, we can just bite the bullet and accept this as a postulant of reasoning. As we will see shortly, we could say, as Hume said, that it is simply an in-built havoc of the human mind. And there is little practical advantage to *not* making that assumption. But, it is important to note that it is an assumption. Every exercise, not only in scientific inductive reasoning but in every day down-home inductive reasoning, every instance of it presumes the uniformity of nature.

Now, even if we simply shelf the problem of trying to prove that induction is legitimate, there are other problems besides that generic rock-bottom problem of induction itself. We need to try to get a handle on what kind of methods can we use when we are generalizing, or when we are going from what has been observed to what has not been observed; what methods? We need to recognize the limitations of the entire apparatus in that it yields probability only, and it never yields certainty. We also need to be alert to the possible flaws of whatever basis that we are carrying out the inductive reasoning is on.

First, something more than a simple enumeration of similarities is called for when we are doing a piece of inductive reasoning or generalizing. If we simply innumerate similarities, and take a flying leap, and say okay on the basis of these similarities, we are home clear. We are using a method that takes no notice of possible disconfirming instances. We are using a method that takes no notice and makes no attempt to provide for undisclosed, undiscovered, or uncontrolled variables.

Let me give you an instance. You could look at a bat and look at a bird, and you would find that bats and birds have many characteristics in common. They are common in their behavior, in their general physiology, their visible external physiology at any rate. It would be very easy to jump to the conclusion on the basis of enumerated similarities between, lets say, bats and crows, to jump to the conclusion that a bat is a kind of bird, which, for the record, is exactly the conclusion Aristotle came to a long time ago. It was not until a great deal of work was done that went beyond those surface or apparent similarities, that brought us to the point of recognizing that bats are mammals, and that they do not belong to the same category in the animal kingdom that birds belong to. So we need to look at our methods.

Secondly, we need to pay attention to the fact that inductive reasoning is probabilistic at best. Why is that the case? Well it amounts to this. If we are saying that if this is a bird then it has these characteristics, and it has these characteristics so it must be a bird—which is the kind of reasoning that Aristotle would have been doing—it is the fallacy of "affirming the consequent" that we have talked about before. If P implies Q, and we can demonstrate that Q is the case, that does not demonstrate that P is the case. It gives it some weight. Now, if P implies Q, and R, and S, and T, and U, and V, and W, and so on, and we can confirm that all of those consequences of P are the case, we may begin to feel very strongly that P itself is the case. But even if we are feeling that very strongly on the basis of many enumerated characteristics, it does not give closure. There is still always the possibility that there is another factor we have not looked at, another characteristic that P implies that is not fulfilled.

And lastly in this connection, we need to be mindful of the fact that even if nature is uniform, it can surprise us. Nature can startle us— not because nature keeps an ace up its sleeve, but mainly because at any point in any individual's life the breadth of our exposure to nature and all of its complexity is severely limited. So there is always the chance that tomorrow we are going to run into that swan that is not white, that tomorrow we are going to run into that politician who is honest and discover that generalizations that we have been comfortable with simply do not work. Our inferences, furthermore, and finally in this context, are no stronger than the basis from which we are inferring. So, if our experiences themselves are unreliable, or ambiguous, or tainted through the presence of some limiting condition with all those kinds of problems that can arise that we have talked about before, then the edifice that we build on those experiences is going to be a house built on sand.

The main thing I want to look at today is the first of these issues. What kind of methods can we use to reason our way from observations to some general claims about that which has not yet been observed? John Stuart Mill lived from 1806 to either 1877 or 1878. John Stuart Mill in his very influential book, *A System of Logic*, laid out—in broad terms—the essential methods of inductive reasoning. And although it is an old book and Mill is an old philosopher, the basic methods that he was talking about way back there in the 19th century are methods that are still honorably and solidly in place. In that book, Mill identified and examined the techniques of what he called the *Method of Agreement*, the *Method of Difference*, the methods of difference and agreement together, the *Method of Residues*, and the *Method of Concomitant Variation*. I want to look at each of those individually and illustrate them with a few simple examples so that we can get a feeling for the methodology that is involved, and how it is more complicated than simply enumerating a number of similarities and taking a flying leap.

Here is how Mill described the Method of Agreement, and I am quoting him: "If two or more instances of the phenomenon under investigation have only one circumstance in common, the circumstance in which alone all of the instances agree, is the cause (or effect) of the given phenomenon in question." We have got a bunch of different situations. They vary from one another. But there is one circumstance that they have in common. Two or more instances have one circumstance in common. That circumstance, that one in which the two incidences agree, is the cause or the effect of the phenomenon in question. An example will make it clear.

Suppose we are having an outbreak of typhoid. And we are trying to figure out why this person, this person, and this person come down with typhoid. What do we go looking for? We go looking for circumstances that they have in common. Now, that circumstance that they have in common might be any number of different things. And we might look to see if they are all getting their water from the same well. No, the source of their well water is not something that they have in common. Do they have this characteristic? No. Do they have that characteristic? No. Have they all had contact with a lady in the neighborhood that I will call Typhoid Mary, with an allusion to history? Well, yes. But, she does not have typhoid. But that is the one thing that they have in common. There must be a link there. That is Mill's point. And let me say in passing that is how we discovered that there are typhoid carriers and not just people who have typhoid or do not have it. There are people who have it, and it does not show. So finding the one thing in common by way of the Method of Agreement is a very useful way to identify a causal connection.

This is Mill's Method of Difference: "If an instance in which the phenomenon under investigation occurs and an instance in which it does not occur, have every circumstance in common, save one, that one occurring only in the former, the circumstance in which alone the two instances differ, is the effect, or the cause, or an indispensable part of the cause of the phenomenon."

Let me tell you a story. This is a story that you may know. And it is a story that I recommend that you look up and read. There was a doctor in Vienna, Dr. Semmelweis, who published a book in1861 about his findings. Dr. Semmelweis was concerned about the death rate of women who had come to the hospital to deliver their children. Dr. Semmelweis noted that the death rate among women who came in for hospital delivery and women whose children were delivered by midwives at home were widely discrepant. The death rate for hospital birthing mothers was off the charts. The death rate for midwife birthing mothers was minimal.

Well, is there anything that is a characteristic of birthing in a hospital that is absent in a midwiving situation? I could stretch the story out, and as I said, look it up. It is a fascinating story. What Semmelweis noted was that the doctors who were doing the deliveries in the hospital were doing so having come directly from their anatomy instruction classes where they were performing autopsies on cadavers. This was something that midwives did not do. He hypothesized that there was some connection between what the doctors were doing in the autopsies and the death of these women. And he proposed a solution, that the doctors wash their hands. This brought down the wrath. He was ridiculed. He was dismissed as a crank. As I said, he published a book enumerating his findings in 1861. Five years later his findings were confirmed by another doctor over in England named Lister, whose name may be more familiar to you. But, in fact, Semmelweis had put his finger on the crucial difference. The difference was contact between doctors and cadavers that was absent between midwives and cadavers. There is where the cause of childbed fever, as it was called, lay.

Now, you can use the methods of agreement and difference together. In fact, we very commonly do just that. We will set up control groups, and we will manipulate the control group and the experimental group, and we will switch roles. Maybe we are giving a trial medicine to an experimental group and giving a placebo to the control group, and after a certain period of time, we will reverse it. What we are doing there is moving the similarities and differences around to see what effect these similarities and differences have. We do that all the time in the testing of pharmaceuticals. It is a standard laboratory practice.

Mill also talks about what he calls the Method of Residues. Here is what he says: "Subtract from any phenomenon such part as is known by previous inductions to be the effect of certain antecedents, and the residue of the phenomenon is the effect of the remaining antecedents." Subtract the parts that you can, and the residue [what is left] is going to be the effect of the residue of the antecedents. Take out what you can already explain, and what you are trying to explain will be covered by whatever data remains.

Let us see if we can illustrate that with a kind of example. I might set up an experiment in my kitchen. I would not call it science. It is just home economics, which we used to call it when I was a lad. I might set up a series of experiments using a microwave oven and making popcorn. Maybe I am trying to figure out what is the reason for the high percentage of duds that I am getting in a particular batch of popcorn that I have bought. And so I experiment with different lengths of time, and with different settings—high, medium, etc. I try doing everything I can to see what can be explained in terms of those. Suppose that what I discover, however, is that with a particular brand of popcorn, I am getting 45 percent duds no matter how long I leave the microwave running, no matter how high I set the setting, no matter whether I have kept the popcorn in a vapor-sealed glass jar from use-to-use. What remains unexplained? A very high level of duds. What factor remains to cover it? The brand. And thus I might, like a home economics specialist working in the kitchens of a consumers union up in New York, I might run a series of tests and identify, by the Method of Residues, that the only way to explain a particular malfunction in the popcorn world has to do with the brand of popcorn that you buy.

I read in the paper just a week or two ago about a very interesting hypothesis that someone has put forward, and that is to the effect that contemporary students in medical school who are learning surgical techniques—they are doing their first autopsies, and they are learning how to wield the knife. They are vastly more adept at this than students were 20 or 25 years ago. The hypothesis that was advanced in the newspaper story about this is that the reason for this quantum leap in finger dexterity has to do with the fact that all of these young would-be surgeons have spent the first 20 years or so of their lives playing video games. They have been madly pushing buttons and getting tense thumbs and all of the things that go with that. I do not know whether that hypothesis is legitimate or not, but my point is, there is a lovely case to try on Mill's Method of Residues. Let us see if we can identify how many different factors might account for some part of this improved dexterity. And let us see if there is a residue left over that we are going to have to explain by playing lots of Pac Man, or Tetris, or whatever, because there is no other way to explain it. It is the Method of Residues.

Lastly, Mill offers what he calls the Method of Concomitant Variation, and I think it is the most important of the lot. Whatever phenomenon varies in any manner, whenever another phenomenon varies in some manner, is either a cause of that phenomenon or is connected with it through some fact of causation—vary this, this varies with it—it might be a directly correlated variation, or it could be inverse. I assisted my wife at one time when our youngest was playing soccer and my wife was coaching. I got roped into being an assistant soccer coach, a soccer dad, I guess. I formulated in those days a hypothesis that if I were in a position to do so, I would check out using Mill's Method of Concomitant Variation. My hypothesis had to do with the connection between the quality of a child's soccer play, whether or not they had ADD, and whether or not they were on their medication. Now just at a casual observational level, it seemed pretty evident to me that children that had been diagnosed with attention deficit disorder and who were not on their medication did not play soccer very well. Those same children, when they were on their medication, did. The presence or absence of the medication was having some direct effect on their quality of play. Now, there is an experiment I never ran, but one that would be very easily established. And aside, it is easier to talk about this kind of thing if we are talking about, lets say, an experiment to discover whether or not variations in the amount of fertilizer that you apply to your lawn has an impact of the growth rate on the grass. Nobody is going to object if we put a little more fertilizer, or put a little less fertilizer, or stress the lawn by not watering.

But some of the most important and serious experimentation that we do falls into the area of human behavior, and the process gets very tricky. That is why at any university when experiments are being done by psychologists, or biologists, or by anybody, experiments must go past a review panel where experiments are very carefully screened to be sure that they do not, in any way, jeopardize the well-being of the experimental subjects, that they recognize the autonomy and the status of the subjects that you are working with, that they have given informed consent, and so on. This means, of course, that it would be, at a practical level, impossible for me to run the kind of experiment I was alluding to a moment ago about juvenile soccer players diagnosed with ADD, on and off their medication. I cannot go in and say that I am going to hide the Ritalin this week and see if the child plays better or plays worse. That would be shocking and intolerable in our community. But you can easily see where that is exactly the kind of thing that is done in pharmaceutical testing, and that is, of course, why we do so much of it at first with laboratory animals. Only after we have done painstaking tests for safety do we would escalate our inductive experimentations into the realm of human subjects and the effects that these things are going to have on human lives.

Well, induction is a wonderful way to *test* a hypothesis, using the methods that we have been talking about. But as we saw at the beginning of the hour, it is no way to *guarantee* that a hypothesis is true. Next time, we will begin to look at hypotheses themselves— where they come from and what we can do with them.

Lecture Fifteen
The Scientific Revolution

Scope:

Early modern scientific thinking depended on powerful mathematical and observational tools and strictly presumed the regularity of nature. For example, using Isaac Newton's concept of reality as "matter in motion" presupposes reliable mathematical techniques for measuring motion, the availability of detailed state descriptions, and the existence of knowable natural laws in terms of which matter's motion can be understood. All three are essential for generating the predictions that are the hallmark of early modern science. Given that Newton denied making hypotheses, one might suppose that the conception of reality, the mathematical apparatus, the natural laws, and the state descriptions that he used must all be reports of, or inferences of one sort or another from, observations. But, as we shall see, this supposition is highly problematic.

Outline

I. Early modern scientific thinking depended on powerful mathematical and observational tools and strictly presumed the regularity of nature.

   A. Isaac Newton conceived of reality as "matter in motion." Making any use of that conception presupposes the availability of a reliable mathematical technique for measuring motion.

   1. Newton himself invented the calculus, and others before him had invented geometry, analytic geometry, and so on.

   2. Contemporary science is strongly mathematical in all its branches, and the mathematical tools involved are not exactly "empirical."

   B. Newton's science also presupposes the availability of detailed state descriptions. That necessitates the availability of reliable observational instrumentation for obtaining the data to be measured.

   1. What is a *state description* in Newtonian science? A state description is an account of a closed physical

system, in which you precisely locate all of the components of that system and precisely identify the direction and momentum of their movement.

2. Why are state descriptions so important? With a state description of a physical system and an understanding of the natural laws that govern that system, we can predict future state descriptions of that same system or, for that matter, retrodict descriptions of that same system at some earlier time.

3. What sort of instruments do we need in order to achieve these accounts? Everything from accurate clocks to the apparatus of modern scientific laboratories.

C. Newton also strictly affirmed the existence of knowable natural laws in terms of which matter's motion can be understood.

1. This invokes the uniformity of nature again.

2. While Newton may have seen natural laws as having a "divine" origin, this is not crucial to the enterprise. They can just as easily be read in "naturalistic" terms.

3. There is one group within the "intelligent design" family, who for theological reasons, denies the uniformity of nature.

II. Mathematical apparatus, precise state descriptions, and natural laws make what we call *understanding* possible. All three of these factors are essential for the generation of the predictions that are the hallmark of modern science.

A. This uniformity and these laws make prediction and retrodiction possible.

B. This all seems to entail (or presume) that "strict causal" determinism is true of the natural order.

C. However, Newton's notion of causation, known as *strict causal determinism*, generates problems.

1. Certain theologians do not want to see divine volitions constrained by anything external.

2. Certain philosophers see problems in the areas of human free will and determinism, as well as human responsibility.

3. Many contemporary physicists, following the work of Heisenberg, dispute the Newtonian notion that nature is, in fact, strictly causally determined.

III. What is the status of "hypotheses" in early modern science? Isaac Newton famously said, "I don't make hypotheses" ("*Hypotheses non fingo.*")

   A. Given that Newton's didn't make hypotheses, one might suppose that the conception of reality, the mathematical apparatus, the natural laws that he "discovered," and the descriptions that he used to generate predictions must all have been direct reports of observations, generalizations of observations, or inferences from those reports and generalizations. Otherwise, where did they come from?

   B. These suppositions are, however, highly problematic.

IV. Consider where mathematical tools come from.

   A. We could make a case that traditional Euclidian geometry is just a generalization from observations by farmers, carpenters, and shipwrights, and the like.

   B. However, for calculus or for Descartes' invention of analytic geometry, which translated geometry into an algebraic system, nothing from the level of observation seems sufficient to generate these tools.

   C. If we did not garner mathematical tools from the world of Platonic Forms and if we did not generalize them from specific observations in this world, then I suggest they come in large part from the inventive genius of individuals who say, "What if?" and then work out the implications of their hypotheses and put them to the test experimentally.

V. Consider where natural laws—or our ideas of natural laws, at least—come from.

   A. Newton's law of universal gravitation states that everything in the universe is impelled by a gravitational force toward everything else in the universe, according to a very precise mathematical formula.

   B. Yet we cannot comfortably say that the law of gravity (or, for that matter, gravity itself) is directly observable.

C. Natural laws are descriptive, and descriptive laws differ from prescriptive ones.

    1. Descriptive laws are very general, detailed, and inclusive accounts of the way the world works. They are not prescriptions of what will, should, or ought to be.

    2. Descriptive laws are revised constantly to make them more and more accurate. Indeed, Newton's law of universal gravitation has been revised numerous times in just that way.

VI. Natural laws, mathematical principles, and state descriptions are not simple observation reports.

    A. Contemporary philosophers of science note the extent to which Newton's (or anyone's) tools, laws, and state descriptions are "colored" by theories that are already in place (that is, they are *theory laden*). We shall examine this matter in Lecture Twenty-Three.

    B. Newton hypothesized his mathematical apparatus and an array of natural laws. Using those hypotheses, he described what he saw in terms of that mathematical and theoretical apparatus.

    C. Looking at Newton from this vantage point, we can observe that when he said, "I make no hypotheses," he was saying that he did not make grand, sweeping, metaphysical, untestable, or bizarre ones—that he tried to keep his hypotheses *grounded*.

Essential Reading:

Samir Okasha, *Philosophy of Science—A Very Short Introduction*.

Recommended Reading:

Irving Copi, *Introduction to Logic*, Chapter 13, "Science and Hypothesis," pp. 493–503.

Questions to Consider:

1. Is it a strength or is it a weakness that scientific explanations are always open to revision in the light of additional data, new hypotheses, and/or refined observations?

2. What do you think is the connection between the various particles, waves, and so on, that physicists talk about and what we can actually observe with our senses?

Lecture Fifteen
The Scientific Revolution

In this and in the two lectures to come, we are going to be looking at the role of "hypotheses" in constructing explanations and accounts of what goes on in the world—not only among scientists but also among police detectives, and also among common everyday folk. As we shall see, hypotheses play a very important role, but we need to talk about where they come from, how we construct them, how we use them, what we can do with them. Preparatory for that, I wanted to say just a bit at the beginning of this session about some characteristics of what I am going to call *scientific inquiry*, but with a little "s." And to make a few comments about the nature of scientific inquiry, I am going to turn our attention briefly to the beginnings of what I will call *early modern science*. We are going to look briefly at what is involved in Sir Isaac Newton's account of scientific investigation. What I hope we will see is that such scientific investigation depends very dramatically on powerful mathematical tools, on powerful observational tools, and—is reminiscent of things we have talked about the last few times—it depends strictly on the assumption that nature itself is uniform.

To make use of the Newtonian idea that nature, reality, amounts to "matter in motion"—that is the key here—to make use of that idea, which goes all the way back to Newton's lifetime, and that is from the mid-17th century to the early 18th century. It presupposes the availability of powerful mathematical tools and powerful mathematical techniques for measuring the matter and the motion. Scientific inquiry, then, is strongly mathematical in all of its branches. Now, it is important to notice that there is a question about the status of those mathematical tools that we use. Where do they come from? Do we discover them? Do we invent them? Do we find them? Do we construct them? Are they "empirically" derived themselves?

I am going to leave that question open for a little while, but I want you to see at the very beginning that there is a question there that needs to be addressed, because if we are going to talk about scientific inquiry as being fundamentally "empirical," we are going to have to provide some kind of room for empirical connections of some kind for the mathematical apparatus that is an essential part of it. An aside: You may have noticed already that I have repeatedly made reference to what I call *modern rational empiricism*. That label is not accidental, for there is a rational side, and there is an empirical side, and they are not identical. End of sidebar. We will come back to that, but we do need to recognize that scientific inquiry is strongly mathematical and that it has a big question mark next to its empirical connections. Newton himself was one of those who was credited with the invention of the calculus—just as others invented—or if you please, discovered or found—geometry, analytic geometry, all of the modern mathematical apparatus that we use in order to measure the quantity of a thing and measure its motion.

Now, scientific inquiry also depends not only upon strong mathematical tools, it also depends on strong observational tools. Without those observational tools, we would not be able to generate an essential part of Newtonian scientific explanation. We would not be able to generate what Newton called "state descriptions." And if we could not generate state descriptions, we would never get this plane off the ground. What do I mean by a state description? What did Newton mean by a state description? A state description is an account of some particular physical system, a closed physical system, in which you locate precisely all of the components of that system and identify precisely the direction and momentum of their movement. Using a classic and flawed model, think of balls on a billiard table, and they are in motion. The cue ball is rolling across the table towards another ball. A state description would be an instantaneous snapshot of where everything is in that closed system, along with an identification of where the ball is headed and with what velocity. Why are state descriptions so important?

Well, the whole notion in Newtonian explanation is that with a state description of a physical system and with an understanding of the natural laws that govern that system, we can then predict future state descriptions of that same system, or, for that matter, retrodict past descriptions of that same system at some earlier time. But, how are we going to get those state descriptions? Not only how could we do it without the math, but how could we do it without the observational techniques that are involved in seeing what is there? It is not hard spotting where the balls are on a billiard table, but it is a little bit tricky to spot where the electrons are in a hydrogen atom. So, life is complicated, and the observational tools that we are talking about are not just relatively simple things, like good clocks. Although if we did not have good clocks, we could not get these things moving. It also involves things like gas spectrometers, whatever they are. I have a friend who uses one of those things, and I find it quite fascinating. But go into any modern scientific laboratory—the apparatus that is in use is directly proportional to the success of the inquiry that is being carried out. If science is observation based, you are going to have to have the observational tools. If it is rational and mathematical in its operations, you are going to have to have the rational and mathematical tools as well.

Finally, as I have said, this whole scientific view of the world strictly presumes the uniformity of nature—that nature is regular, that nature rolls on inevitably.

Now Newton described the uniformity of nature in terms of "divine" laws. He dressed up natural laws in terms of divine edicts, and that is perfectly all right. It does not make any difference to what is crucially at issue here, and that is, again, the notion that nature itself is uniform.

Let me digress for a moment. I have just recently been doing a lot of reading in the context of the controversy between evolutionary theory and what has recently been called *intelligent design theory* about the origins of life and the development of human life. I suggest that there is a vast literature out there that would be quite interesting for you to have a look at. But one of the things that I discovered is that there is one group within the intelligent design family who, for theological reasons, deny the uniformity of nature. They deny the existence of natural laws on the grounds that the uniformity of nature, or the existence of natural laws, would constrain the free volitions of the divine power. Well, I do not know quite what to make of that myself, but I certainly know what Newton would have made of it. He would have seen that this was absolutely antithetical to the enterprise that he was trying to engage in. The enterprise that he was engaging in was an enterprise predicated upon the existence of a reliable, discoverable, and knowable natural order articulated in natural laws.

So, all three of these factors—mathematical apparatus, precise state descriptions, and natural laws—are essential for the generation of the predictions, the foresight, and the explanations that are the lifeblood of modern scientific inquiry. They are what make prediction possible. They are what make what we call "understanding" possible.

One last quick aside: We have been talking a lot about the regularity of nature, and I have been talking about Newton's reliance on the notion that things that occur in nature are "strictly causally" connected—locked, strict causation. The label for that in the philosophical community is causal determinism or "strict causal" determinism. Well, I just want to note in passing that they not only may make a few problems for certain theologians who do not want to see divine volitions constrained by anything external, but the whole question of strict causation also poses problems for philosophers in the area of the question of human free will and, consequently, in the issue of human responsibility for the things that we do.

For if the Newtonian account is correct, if we had a state description of nature—we don't—but if we had a state description of nature, say, in 1066, at the Battle of Hastings, and if we understood all the laws that govern nature's events—which we don't, but if we did—if we had that state description and had all of those laws in-hand and understood them, and if we had the mathematical apparatus that we needed to have to work with it, we would have been able to predict, in principle, 20 years ago that I would be standing here today saying what I am saying and worrying you with the question of whether or not human behavior is ever genuinely free or creative, or is simply the causal output of events long gone.

Now there is an enormous problematical area that is not our proper business here, now, in this course. Go on the Web; look up free will and determinism, and you will find a literature that will keep you busy for decades. Let me also notice that in contemporary science following the work of Heisenberg and other contemporary physicists, we have come to the point of calling severely into question the Newtonian notion that nature is strictly causally determined. We are going to come back to that later on in this series of lectures because the possibilities that are involved in Heisenberg's indeterminacy theory in changing the whole way that we look at the world, the whole way that we explain phenomenon that occur in the world, are among those things to which we will give attention.

So, science relies upon mathematical and observational tools. It relies on the assumption that nature is strongly uniform, that laws can be "discovered" in terms of which we can make predictions and understand what is going on in the world. To do that, I want to argue that we have to construct and offer hypotheses in order to get the explanatory enterprise moving. I would not think that this was a problematic claim on my part, save for the fact that Isaac Newton very famously said, "I don't make hypotheses." My pronunciation of Latin is atrocious, but that comes out something like *Hypotheses non fingo*. "I don't make them," says Newton. Well, how then was Newton able to put into place the observation and the mathematical analysis and the principle of the uniformity of nature and the reliability of natural laws? Where does that all come from? Where does it all come from if it is not hypothesized, tried on for size, and then weighed inductively to see whether it is more or less probable? Specifically, consider the mathematical tools that science uses, which we use in everyday affairs and that Newton himself used.

Now you could make a kind of a case that traditional Euclidian geometry is just a generalization from observations that we have made. We simply observe that the square of the hypotenuse is equal to the sum of the squares of the other two legs. Well, we can say that, and at a stretch, I am suggesting that that is plausible. Indeed, I would not be surprised if we were never in a position to do the historical inquiry; it would take a time machine to do it. But I would not be surprised if we were not to discover that a great many of those ancient home truths of Euclidian geometry were just generalizations from the observations of farmers, carpenters, shipwrights, and all of the people who were working with acreage, or working with tools to build things.

What about the calculus? What about Descartes's invention of analytic geometry, translating geometry over into an algebraic system? What reason would anyone have at the level of observation to think that geometry could be repackaged in algebraic equations other than to hypothesize that something along this line might work? Work at it; try it a bit; and see where you can get with it.

Now there are other possibilities. Maybe the mathematics that we work with is something that we recall from a previous existence when our mind is in direct communion with the forms. You will remember that is what Plato suggested. I see no strong reason to think that Plato was right. The only thing that I see a strong reason for accepting is the fact that we do have a powerful mathematical apparatus in-hand that is teachable, understandable, and fruitful.

Well, if we did not garner it from the world of the forms, and if we did not generalize it from specific observations in this world, whence then did it come? I am suggesting to you that it comes in large part—and I am going to use a phrase that I will be using several times in the next several sessions—it comes in large part from the inventive genius of individuals who see things in a different way, those who say, "What if?" But they do not just say "What if?" and then spin fantasies. They say "What if?" and then they work out the implications of their hypotheses and put them to the test experimentally.

And where do the natural laws come from? Where does our idea of the natural laws come from? Consider Newton's law of universal gravitation, that everything in the universe is impelled by a gravitational force towards everything else in the universe, according to a very precise mathematical formula. Well, nobody ever saw gravity, or tasted it, or smelled it, and you might want to say they felt it, but I would question that. I feel the weight of a package that I am carrying. I infer that the weight that I am feeling is because of the gravitational force that is working on that package, pulling it towards the earth against the resistance of my arms. But the gravitation business that comes in there comes in the explanatory hypothesis that is being offered to explain what is felt, which is resistance against my muscles.

So, I do not think we can comfortably say that the natural laws on which the enterprise so heavily relies are themselves directly observable, and surely they are not something that we ran into in the world of the forms. One hesitates to say that they are simply invented because, of course, if we could just invent them at will, then—in a sense—we could make them what we wanted them to be, and the world does not work that way. The natural laws that we articulate and state are attempts to describe the way things operate.

I have said "natural laws" in the last five minutes. I need to put a flag and a warning here. The word "law" is a word over which dangerous equivocation can easily happen because there are what we call "descriptive laws," and there are what we call "prescriptive laws," which are not the same thing. They are not the same thing at all. To talk about nature being governed by natural laws is really quite misleading. That makes it sound as though we are talking about edicts that have been enacted, and that nature perhaps restively, or with resentment, is bowing under the weight of those edicts that have been imposed. Descriptive laws are what we are talking about when we talk about natural laws. They are simply detailed accounts of the way the world works. Natural laws are very general and inclusive descriptions. They are not prescriptions of what will, should, or ought to be. And I can illustrate that very simply by noting the difference between our reaction if we find that a natural law has been "violated," and our reaction if a prescriptive law has been violated.

If I get out on I-95 this evening and drive 100 miles an hour toward Petersburg, all of you can hope for your mutual safety that the highway patrol will stop me, and that being in violation of the speed laws of the Commonwealth of Virginia, that I will get a healthy fine and maybe lose my license. I will be punished for breaking the law. What if we discovered that two things in space were accelerating towards one another—not at a rate that was inversely proportional to the square of the distance between them, but according to some other formula? Well, I will tell you what we would not do. We would not get out the whips and punish those two things that were not obeying the law. What we would do is say, "Whoops! We misdescribed." The law gets restated. Descriptive laws are revised constantly to make them descriptively more and more accurate, and Newton's law of universal gravitation has been revised numerous times in just that way.

So, for the laws and the mathematics, and I would say for the state descriptions themselves, these things are not simple observations or simple generalizations of simple observations. When we describe a state of affairs, all kinds of theoretical dimensions come into the very description that we use. We will talk more of this later because one of the great concerns in contemporary accounts of scientific reasoning is the extent to which even the simplest descriptions are what is called "theory laden." We will be talking about that in Lecture Twenty-three, way down at the end of the course. Well, perhaps then, when Newton said, "I don't make hypotheses," perhaps he was engaging in a bit of hyperbole. I think, in fact, Newton made hypotheses right and left. He hypothesized a mathematical apparatus; he hypothesized an array of natural laws. Using those, he described what he saw in terms of that mathematical and theoretical apparatus in place, and then he offered us an expanding, growing network of explanatory muddles and explanatory principles in terms of which to try to understand what is going on in the world. He hypothesized right and left. Perhaps, then, what he did mean when he said, "I make no hypotheses" was simply that he did not make grand, or sweeping, or metaphysical, or untestable, or bizarre hypotheses—that he tried to keep his hypotheses grounded. And if that is what he meant, he was making a very serious and important point. If our hypotheses are not grounded or connected in some way to what we can observe and work with at a direct level, then they can lead us on a merry chase into foolishness.

Now, to look at Newton that way and to say, as he says, "I make no hypotheses," he is saying I am confining myself to hypotheses that are grounded and testable. I am reading back into Newton a great deal of post-Newtonian history of science and philosophy of science. I am looking at Newton more or less from the vantage point of what in the mid-20th century we would have called *logical empiricism*. So there is anticipation there, again, of something that we will turn to very shortly when we describe—give a state description if you would like of it—normal science in the mid-20th century.

Lecture Sixteen
Hypotheses and Experiments—A First Look

Scope:

If important theories and laws, and even the existence of the entities and forces they are "about," can't be inferred from our observations, then something like hypothesis construction (or invention) will have to have a place in explanatory thinking. *What* place to make for it in science has been disputed, raising issues about whether (and, if so, how) scientific inquiry is genuinely empirical. Irresponsible hypothesis construction, after all, is hard to distinguish from mere speculation. Responsible hypothetical inquiry is grounded in testing and experimentation—a dialectic of hypothesis and counterexample. Hypotheses that are grounded and confirmed in this way generate covering laws. Covering laws provide the building blocks for state descriptions and testable predictions.

Outline

I. If scientific inquiry were limited to describing and trying to explain macro-level observations, then we might be able to make a somewhat plausible case for a methodology that boils down to observation and simple elaboration, or generalization, based on it.

    A. That might work for certain kinds of biological or botanical classification and taxonomy. It might work for kitchen science.

    B. However, a great many of the things that scientists have the most to say about are things that we have never in any sense directly observed.

II. If important theories and laws, and even the existence of the entities and forces they are "about," can't be inferred from our observations, then something like the construction or invention of hypotheses will have to have a place in explanatory thinking.

III. This is equally true of both scientific and "everyday" explanations. But while the need for hypotheses in both venues is obvious, the precise role and status of a hypothesis in a scientific explanation has long been a topic of debate.

    A. We cannot "infer" that the Sun will rise tomorrow from our observation that it has risen every day that we can remember. We can (and do) expect that it will do so, but that is part habit, part hope, and all hypothetical.

    B. Nor can we "infer" that atomic nuclei can be fused from any observations of atomic nuclei that we have ever had. Indeed, given that we have never observed even one atomic nucleus, the difficulty here is not just the "problem of induction."

    C. Thus, we (somehow) construct or invent hypotheses, entertain the supposition that they are true, and on that supposition, infer the possibility of particular fusions from the hypothesis package itself. The inference is *from* the hypothesis, not *to* it.

IV. The use of invented hypotheses in constructing a scientific explanation raises an issue: If the hypotheses themselves are not derived from observations, then in what sense is a scientific explanation that employs them "empirical"?

    A. Irresponsible hypothesis construction is, after all, hard to distinguish from mere speculation.

        Negative example: Erich von Daniken's *Chariots of the Gods*.

    B. Intemperate hypothesis construction violates Ockham's Razor.

        1. One should never hypothesize more than is needed.

        2. This is also known as *theoretical economy* or *parsimony*.

    C. Rational empiricists, consequently, have a healthy mistrust of untested (and especially *untestable*) hypotheses about matters of fact.

D. Rational empiricists insist that responsible explanations are always grounded, somehow, in testing and experimentation—a dialectic of hypothesis and counterexample as old as Socrates but still at the core of things.

E. That testing, however, is *indirect*. We test the *output* of the hypothesis, theory, or explanation, not the thing itself.

F. Successful testing, then, does not prove a hypothesis true (that is the fallacy of affirming the consequent), but unsuccessful tests can defeat a hypothesis. Accumulated successes are said to "support" a hypothesis or "lend it weight."

G. As famously noted by such scientists as Albert Einstein and such philosophers as Karl Popper and Carl Hempel, this *empirical connection* is, curiously, "after the fact." We will examine some of the implications of this in Lectures Seventeen and Eighteen.

H. Output testing (that is, experimentation) is not only a check on our idle fancies, but it can also reveal opportunities for new hypotheses and, hence, new avenues of research.

I. When several hypotheses have been advanced and experimentally confirmed, they can be woven together into progressively more inclusive explanatory tapestries as theories, laws, and covering laws.

Essential Reading:

Carl Hempel, *Philosophy of Science,* Chapter 5, "Laws and Their Role in Scientific Explanation," pp. 47–69.

Recommended Reading:

Irving Copi, *Introduction to Logic*, Chapter 13, "Science and Hypothesis," pp. 504–522.

Questions to Consider:

1. If our hypotheses "color" the way in which we perceive the results of our experiments, does this mean that our experiments are irretrievably tainted? How can experimental output help us

"correct" a hypothesis if that output is filtered by the hypothesis in question?

2. What are the relative merits of the two following "explanations" of rain in central Virginia?

   (a) "It rained because the confluence of cold air moving southeastward from Alberta and moist warm air moving westward off the Atlantic caused the ambient temperature of the atmosphere over central Virginia to drop below the dew point."

   (b) "It rained because the Chickahominy elders performed a rain dance."

Lecture Sixteen
Hypotheses and Experiments—A First Look

If scientific inquiry were limited to describing and trying to explain macro-level, big, observable stuff, then we might be able to make a somewhat plausible case for the notion that its methodology boils down to observation and simple elaboration, or generalization, from what is observed, and that might work for certain kinds of biological or botanical classification and taxonomy, and so on. It might work for kitchen science of the sort that we all practice as we are trying to make a better pan of biscuits, one of my hobbies. One of the difficult things, though, is that when we look at the way Science is practiced, capital "S" now, we find that a great many of the things that the scientists have the most to say about are things that we have never in any sense directly observed. And if we have never observed those things at all, then the problem that we have in methodology is not just a problem of perhaps too hastily generalizing from observations in-hand. How do you too hastily, or even not too hastily, generalize observations that you have never had?

My point is that as Science has turned its attention to the micro level, and as Science has become more and more abstract, it has not become less and less useful. It has become more and more useful, but its relationship to its empirical underpinnings and its empirical foundations seems more and more tenuous, more and more difficult to pin down and understand. To say that more tightly: If important Scientific theories and laws, and even the existence of the entities that those theories and laws are "about," cannot be observed themselves and cannot be directly inferred from what we do observe, then something like the invention or construction of explanatory hypotheses will have to have a place in Scientific thinking. Now, I think this is equally true of both capital "S" Science and of everyday, lower-case "s" scientific explanations as well.

But while the need for hypotheses and the construction of them in both venues is obvious to me, the precise role and precise status of those hypotheses in capital "S" Scientific explanations is a topic of long and heated debate. So let us back up a step. I am suggesting, and I suggested several lectures back, that we cannot directly "infer" even that the sun will rise tomorrow from our observation that the sun has risen every day so far that we can remember. We can and we do expect that the sun will rise tomorrow, but as we have seen, that is part habit, part hope, and very hypothetical. Much more problematic than that, however, is the fact that we cannot "infer" anything about, let us say, atomic nuclei. Let us say that they can be fused in a hydrogen bomb. We cannot infer that from any observation of atomic nuclei that we have ever had, for the simple reason that we have never observed one—not even one.

The difficulty here, then, is not just the "problem of induction"—it is not just the problem of trying to constrain our haste in extrapolating too far on the basis of limited observational data. Here we are not merely generalizing observations with all of the attendant risks that go with that. We are generalizing the behavior of unobservables, the existence of which are simply a hypothetical offering on our own part. Now perhaps you can see why I say that the empirical underpinnings, the empirical connections of scientific explanations when we get to this level, are tenuous. They are very hard to locate and very hard to pin down.

What we are going to see, however, is that the empirical connection can be made in terms of the output of the hypothesis that we offer. The empirical connection is not going to be made in terms of the source of the hypothesis that we offer. There will be more on that momentarily.

So, we somehow construct or invent a hypothesis. We entertain the supposition that it is true. On that entertainment we then deduce. We carry out a rational process of figuring out what will be the outcome. What will be the results if that hypothesis was correct in a situation of this kind? What would be the outcome or the results that we can observe or test at an experimental observational level? So, we cannot extrapolate from our observations of fusing nuclei to the general claim about the possibility of a nuclear weapon. But we might hypothesize the existence of certain sub-atomic particles arranged in certain fashions, and on the basis of that hypothesis and a wide family of other understanding already in place, we might then work our way into the position of being able to predict that certain phenomena will occur under certain circumstances that are explained or are only understandable or are best in terms of the hypothesis that we have put forward. The inference then is *from* the hypothesis to predictable outcome. The inference is not from observations *to* the hypothesis.

Now, this is a dangerous enterprise. Remember, just a couple of lectures back we were talking about the dreadful danger of presuming facts not in evidence. And interestingly enough, every time we come up with a novel, new, inventive, or explanatory hypothesis, we are entertaining the possibility of the reality of certain states of affairs that is not in evidence. So if our hypothesis construction is going to be responsible at all, it is going to have to be held on a very tight leash of after-the-fact confirmation and testing. Remember all the while that when we do after-the-fact confirmation and testing of a hypothesis or a prediction of any kind, the fulfillment that we obtain if we obtain it, gives us only some level of probable correctness for the hypothesis in place.

Now, this raises some issues. Irresponsible hypothesis construction, after all, is going to be very hard to distinguish from mere speculation. Intemperate hypothesis construction is going to be very, very hard to distinguish from wild violations of an old principle called "Ockham's Razor." Let me say what I mean by irresponsible hypothesis construction and intemperate hypothesis construction and a bit about Ockham's Razor, as well. Let me give you an example. There was a fascinating book entitled *Chariots of the Gods* that was published quite some years ago now by a man named (Erich) von Daniken. What von Daniken was offering in that book was an attempt to explain certain observable phenomena that all of us can plainly see. The pyramids on the Yucatan Peninsula, for example; the flattened top of certain mountains in the Andes, for example; the inscriptions that are on some of those pyramids, for example. And let me say that the pyramids in the Yucatan are fascinating; I have been there. I have climbed the pyramids. I have seen the inscriptions, and I am intrigued by what is there. And I have felt my own curiosity being peaked to ask, "How did all of this come about? Why do we have pyramids in the Yucatan? For that matter, why do we have some flattened mountain tops in the Andes?" Well, von Daniken came up with an absolutely marvelous explanation: extraterrestrial visitors. The extraterrestrial visitors came down in spaceships, flying saucers. They taught the indigenous people of the Yucatan how to build pyramids. They came in with intergalactic style, earth-moving equipment far beyond the technology of early human times and flattened off those mountain tops. Why, you ask? Why flatten the mountain top? So as to have a place to park your flying saucer, of course!

Here is a wonderful package of speculations, a wonderful package of hypothesized presumptions about what might have happened, which if they had happened would help us understand some of the things that we observe today. Now, we need to find a way to honestly and fairly distinguish between that kind of hypothesis construction and a kind of hypothesis construction that is going on when Einstein proposes his general theory of relativity. Believe me, there are things mentioned in Einstein's general theory of relativity that are even more obscure than the notion of little green men in flying saucers flattening the tops of mountains so that they will have a place to land, as well as teaching the locals how to build pyramids.

So, one of the things we are going to have to be looking at very closely is how do we distinguish between responsible hypothesis construction and wild speculation. I said to you last time that Sir Isaac Newton was quite famous for having claimed that he made no hypotheses. I offered a spin on that statement, and let me return to that for a moment to say that I think what he meant was that he does not make that kind of wild, speculative, untestable, hypothesis. Testability is going to be crucially central to everything where we draw a distinction between responsible and irresponsible hypothesis construction.

The other thing I wanted to mention at this point was Ockham's Razor because I made reference to Ockham. Ockham lived in the late 13th century to the mid-14th century. I think he died around 1349 or 1350. Ockham made a wonderful contribution to the history of philosophy, science, and wisdom in general—and that is, that one should never hypothesize more than is needed. One should try to keep one's hypothesis construction on a short leash. So, if I am trying to explain, and this is an actual anecdote from von Daniken's book, if I am trying to explain a peculiar metallic, hollow object that I find in the middle of the scrub that is called jungle in the Yucatan, then I do not have to go all the way to the level of extraterrestrial visitors, spaceships, and all the rest of it. I could go only so far as careless tourists who discarded some metal flashlight batteries a few weeks ago that have corroded in the local atmosphere. And in opting for the corroding batteries hypothesis to explain what I am observing, in preference to the extraterrestrial visitors hypothesis to explain what I am observing, I would be siding with Ockham. I would be siding with what is called "theoretical economy," or siding with what is called "parsimony"—that is, not hypothesizing any more than absolutely having to in order to deal with the data at hand.

Rational empiricists have a very healthy mistrust of untested hypotheses, and they have a dramatic mistrust of *untestable* hypotheses. My good friend Jim Rachels, a moral philosopher and a colleague of many years who died recently, used to chide me rather aggressively on occasion for what he called "speculating about matters of fact." And he would say, "Why in the world speculate about matters of fact? All in the world that you have to do is just wait; we will see; do not speculate." But it is such fun. It is so entertaining to dream up possible accounts, which if they were true would explain whatever it is we are observing. But it is so easy to fall into the trap of irresponsibility.

Pursue this one step further. All of you, just like me, know someone who subscribes to what we call "the conspiracy theory of history." And there have been lots of conspiracy theories of history depending upon which particular person you are talking to. I can understand that. I do not do it relative to the broad sweep of history myself, but I find myself doing the same kind of thing in trying to understand faculty politics, or trying to understand the relationship between my youngest son and his girlfriend. And I can fancifully imagine the presence of some dark Lord of Sith who is manipulating history and making things happen this way, or making things happen that way. But it is a very irresponsible enterprise.

When an unfortunately large number of students at Chapel Hill committed suicide back in the 1960s, a book was published there explaining all of this as the direct work of the International Communist Conspiracy. The title of the book was *Blood on the Old Well*, written by Steven and Sarah Emery, one of my teachers at one time, historically. It was so enveloping and so all inclusive that there was, according to that book, a chain of command that ran directly from the Kremlin to the United Nations in New York, to the White House, and from the White House to the governor's mansion in Raleigh, and from the governor's mansion to the chancellor of UNC Chapel Hill, and from the chancellor to the janitors who worked in the various dormitories, and who were busily assassinating various students and then dressing it up to be a wave of suicides.

Well, how do you distinguish between responsible hypothesis construction and irresponsible hypothesis construction? One standard way is to appeal to Ockham's Razor. Do not hypothesize more than you need to in order to explain the data at hand. The other sorts of things that you are going to want to do is to see whether or not the hypothesis that you have come up with ties in comfortably, rationally, and coherently with the existing body of explanation, scientific principles, and laws that are already in place. Is it coherent? Does it mesh? Is it fertile? There are quite a number of things that we have talked about previously and will talk about more.

But in all of this, we are going to be taking that hypothesis, figuring out what it implies, and then looking to see whether or not those implications are confirmable at the level of observation. If there were an international conspiracy in place with tentacles that reached from the Kremlin directly to the janitor's room in Old East, would not there be some implications of that, that one would expect to be discoverable? By wire-tapping and by following the janitor, we can put our ingenuity to mind trying to figure out how could we test the hypothesis in place. And I think if we did that, we would very quickly find that the hypothesis in place has many implications that are not fulfilled, along with the one implication that it does have that is fulfilled—namely that several students took their own lives.

So it is not an impossible task to weigh in and use a hypothesis that has been put forward, to see whether or not it bears fruit when we put it to work. But notice that testing is indirect. We do not just hold up the hypothesis and say, "Where does this correspond directly to what we observe?" We set up a kind of dialectic here, if you please. And we have mentioned dialectic at several points over the course of these lectures, a notion that goes all the way back to Plato and Socrates. This is a particular kind of dialectic where the hypothesis offers predictions. The predictions are tested at the observational level.

What do the results of that testing do? They modify the hypothesis that we are working with. It is a dialogue that goes on between the hypothesis offered, implications drawn out, implications tested and confirmed, implications tested and disconfirmed, and hypotheses that are modified, fine-tuned, and improved—and that is an indirect process and a complex one. Notice again, successful testing in that dialogue does not ever prove with closure that the hypothesis in question is correct. The larger the network of output that is confirmed, the more and more secure we are entitled to feel about the hypothesis that is in place.

But there is always the possibility that the next experimental run is going to reveal the presence of a variable that we have not previously noticed and had not controlled for. It is going to yield an anomalous piece of output. So, however probable we may be secure in saying that a particular hypothesis is, given the present level of experimentation, and exploration, and understanding, the scientific thinker—capital "S" or little "s" now, either one—the person who is thinking scientifically is always going to be ready at a moment's notice to modify the hypothesis, to improve the hypothesis, to make the hypothesis better, and then keep that dialogue going. It is a never-ending task. So our hypotheses get "support" or they go down in flames, but they never, ever get proved. So, as is very famously noted by Albert Einstein in the mid-20th century, and by Karl Popper, and by Hempel, and by dozens of other people in that era, the "empirical connection" of scientific inquiry is "after the fact." The empirical connection of scientific inquiry is an output connection, not a source connection, as we will see when we examine scientific empiricism even more closely in Lectures Seventeen and Eighteen.

Now, that output testing experimentation has another interesting role to play, however. It not only acts as a check on our idle fancies, or a check on our more robust and fanciful speculations. I think that output testing also, and perhaps most importantly, reveals dimensions to the data. It reveals dimensions to the situation we are trying to explain; that opens up the possibility for new hypotheses, new questions, new insights, and new avenues of research. I once read of a man in the 17th century or so who committed suicide and left a note saying that he was ending it all because there was nothing left to discover. "Everything is known, nothing exciting to do with my life, stop the world, I am getting off." And we look back at that and think, how ludicrous. We look at the incredible vista of discoveries, and expanding knowledge, and understanding that have happened since then. But, if we look ahead rather than look back, presuming the uniformity of nature, I admit it, we see a continually opening vista of discoveries to be made. There are new avenues, new directions in which research can be taken, new understandings to be found.

I think we live in exciting times, and one of the reasons that we live in exciting times is because we are laymen and capital "S" Scientists alike. We are committed to a dialectical enterprise of hypothesis construction and testing that is perpetually open-ended.

Now, when a particular hypothesis has been advanced and experimentally confirmed, and it works, and other hypotheses are advanced and experimentally confirmed, and they work, we then begin to weave these together into larger explanatory tapestries, covering laws. Now, there is argument about hypothesis, theory, law, covering law. What I would like for you to see is that there is a continuum there—that the grandest and most complete covering law of modern physics is nothing more than what has grown out of a network of tentative hypotheses advanced, put to the test, and tentatively confirmed.

Lecture Seventeen
How Empirical Is Modern Empiricism?

Scope:

At the macro level, direct observations and inferences from them (that is, generalizations and extrapolations) are possible. Inquiry that is thus *based on* empirical data is *genetically* empirical. At the micro level, however, and at the theoretical and abstract level, a different kind of empirical link is required. Here, that link is to the *testable output* of the hypotheses rather than to their *sources*. Such inquiry is *confirmationally* empirical. One interesting implication of this is that the pedigree of hypotheses becomes epistemically less important than tradition had held. This opens the door to theoretical imagination, creativity, and conceptual invention, but it also keeps our potentially speculative excursions empirically connected in terms of what can demonstrably be done with them.

Outline

I. At the macro level, direct observations and inferences from them are possible, if not foolproof.

   A. Direct observations are crucial and available when considering such matters as the concomitant variation of fertilizer use and crop yield.

   B. Generalizations and extrapolations from observations are exactly the thing if we are trying to decide whether to expand an agricultural practice that has been useful.

   C. Possible problems arise of course. We can mis-see, misconstrue, and mis-infer. Indeed, all of the fallacies are possible, especially hasty generalization.

   D. Inquiry that is thus *based on* empirical data is *genetically* empirical.

   E. Through the first third of the 20th century, there was a controversy among philosophers of science about whether science had to be *genetically* empirical at every point, that is, about whether every scientific claim must be rooted in observations.

II. At the micro level, however, where we may have no direct observations to generalize, a different kind of empirical link is required.

   A. Here, since we have no direct observations, there is nothing to generalize or extrapolate. We can use $e = mc^2$ to calculate the energy of an atomic reaction, but never having directly observed the reference of e, m, or c, or any atoms, we don't get that formula inductively.

   B. Thus, we have to hypothesize general principles, rather than infer them. This is exactly what was done to arrive at $e = mc^2$.

   C. The link here must be to the *testable output* of the hypotheses, not to their *sources*. Such inquiry is *confirmationally* rather than *genetically* empirical.

      1. This amounts to what A. J. Ayer called "indirect verification" in *Language, Truth and Logic.*

      2. With $e = mc^2$, of course, that output is *plainly* observable.

   D. This requires that a hypothesis be in place. You cannot test what you have not hypothesized. But it says *nothing* about where the hypothesis is to be obtained.

      1. Call it inspiration, luck, or genius, we are eternally indebted to the contributions of a Newton or Semmelweis.

      2. Most of us spend our time working out the implications of those insights, testing them, modifying them, working with them, exploring in terms of them.

   E. The empirical connections of the hypotheses' output may not be obvious without the help of mathematics, complex instrumentation, and very creative "supplementary" or "bridging" hypotheses.

      1. You cannot confirm a hypothesis about radiation by using a Geiger counter unless you have a Geiger counter and all of the subsidiary information, protocols, and theories that make one useful.

      2. It is not just a flash of insight. Perhaps 99 percent of the scientific work comes between the insight and the output.

   F. Possible problems arise, of course.

1. For hypotheses-in-hand, the main problems center on how to decide between rivals.
2. This is where coherence, mesh, scope, fertility, capacity for self-correction, the breadth of data covered, mesh with other theories, and the like, as noted in Lecture Nine, come into play (along with Ockham's Razor).
3. Deciding between alternative hypotheses is typically a pragmatic decision procedure—seeking something that works, both in terms of the quality and reliability of the output that comes out of the theory and of the productivity of the theory as compared to its rivals.
4. For scientists, police detectives, and dimwitted spouses, however, the main problem may be in coming up with any hypothesis at all.

III. On this view, as Einstein famously noted, the pedigree of hypotheses is of far less epistemic importance than tradition had held.

A. Confirmational empiricism opens the door to theoretical imagination, creativity, and conceptual invention. This is the venue not only for creative geniuses but also for ordinary folk who pay very close attention to what they *do* observe and have the ability to *make* connections where connections cannot be seen.

B. But confirmational empiricism also keeps our potentially speculative excursions empirically connected in terms of what can demonstrably be done with them.

C. That "connection" is why experimentation in general, and good experimental method in particular, are so important. We shall look at this closely in Lecture Eighteen.

Essential Reading:

Carl Hempel, *Philosophy of Science*, Chapter 2, "Scientific Inquiry: Invention and Test."

Recommended Reading:

Lewis White Beck, "Constructions and Inferred Entities."

Philipp G. Frank, "Einstein, Mach and Logical Positivism."

Questions to Consider:

1. In the model of an atom on my desk, the electrons are green. What color are real electrons?

2. We know that aspirin works for headaches, whether it really prevents heart attacks or not. But we may wonder why it works for headaches. According to a childhood neighbor, it is "because it has something in it." Is any better account than that available?

Lecture Seventeen
How Empirical Is Modern Empiricism?

We were talking about the place of hypothesis construction and experimentation in modern empirical rational inquiry in our last session, and we are going to be continuing that this time and the next time as well. I want to look at this broad question about modern rational empiricism. Just how empirical is it? How, and where, and in what fashion, and to what extent is the empirical side of rational empirical inquiry solid and well-established?

At the everyday level, and even at the technical level, when we are talking about macro-sized objects, direct observations and inferences from them are perfectly possible. That is not to say they are foolproof, but they certainly are available to us. And let us think about that for just a moment in terms of a few very concrete examples.

For instance, if we are considering such a matter as how much fertilizer we want to use on the lawn, direct observation is crucial, and it is available. Or, at a slightly grander scale, if we are considering different maneuvers that we could try in order to increase our crop yield if we were engaged in the farming business, and as we pursued that, the things that we need to keep track of are right there before our eyes, so to speak. We can observe them. We can keep records on them. We can very carefully, following Mills's method of noncombatant variation, raise the level of fertilizer use and make a record of the effect, and then lower it and make a record of that. And, of course, along the way, we can keep track of other variables that strike us in terms of the experience that we have already had as being reasonably relevant to what is going on here. So we would not only want to track the amount of our fertilizer use, but we are also going to want to track the amount and kind of irrigation that we are using. Are we doing aerial spray irrigation, or are we doing trickle irrigation in the furrows, and so on? But all of these things are perfectly, straightforwardly observable. We can work with them. There is no question about empirical linkages there.

Generalizations and extrapolations from an experience are just the thing when we are trying to make those kinds of decisions, and fertilizer use is not the only one. I am in an agricultural mood for the moment, but think about decisions that farmers have made over the years, perhaps as the result of an accidental discovery. But then generalize on the basis of that accident, and what I am thinking of is contour plowing, where the farmer perhaps has plowed his land without any particular plan. He has noticed that where the furrows follow the contour lines, the erosion is significantly less. He is not losing his seed crop every time there is a gully washer rain. Extrapolating from that, the next time he plows he follows that plan throughout, and he does much better. Similarly, with crop rotation, there are all kinds of agricultural practices, which in the 19th century interestingly enough were called scientific farming. There are all kinds of agricultural practices that came directly out of observation, generalization and extrapolation from what we have observed, and the trial then of some general new pattern to confirm or disconfirm the utility of going that route.

I want to call principles that are empirical, *genetic empiricism*—that is, the empirical connection is to its roots, to its *sources*. You start with experience, and the principles grow out of that.

Historical footnote: Even through the first-third of the 20th century, there was a large school of thought among philosophers of science who wanted to insist that science had to be *genetically* empirical at every point. Every scientific claim had to be rooted in observations. We will see.

At the micro level we run into a different kind of situation. Here, perhaps, we have no direct observations to generalize, nothing to extrapolate from. Consider Einstein's proposal that $e = mc^2$. The energy is equal to the mass, times a constant that is the speed of light squared. Where did that come from? Who observed see, taste, smell, feel, hear, energy, mass, or the speed of light? Or, for that matter, who observed the reference of the superscript that says squared in our mathematical conventions? Einstein certainly did not notice, so to speak, out in the garden one day that energy in that system is equal to the mass of the system times the speed of light squared. The next day he did not, while working on his car, discover the energy of the carburetor, and I will generalize from that. No, he had a creative flash, let us say, just for the moment. We will discuss more about that later. But what I want to urge upon you is the notion that $e = mc^2$ is just as empirical as contour plowing reduces runoff in rainstorms is empirical. It is just empirical in a different direction. What happens here at the micro level is that the hypothesis frequently has to be offered ahead of the observations. The hypothesis actually structures and sets up the frame of reference, the perspective in terms of which observations are going to get made.

Consider two people in a laboratory. One of them is me, naïve and inexperienced in laboratory matters. The other is a rocket scientist. I venture to say that as I look at the readings, and the printouts, and all of the data that is being generated in that laboratory—hear me carefully—I do not see what the scientist sees because I am not looking at it with the scientist's eyes. More importantly, I am not looking at it with the scientist's conceptual apparatus. All of the ideas and theories are in place in terms of which the scientist construes the bits and pieces of data that are coming in, in terms of a hypothesis that is already in place.

So, if there is going to be an empirical link for this kind of work, it is not going to be genetic. It cannot be. It is going to have to be somewhere else. And that is why I was anticipating last time. That is why mid-century and later philosophers of science and scientists, people who write about scientific method, have talked so much about the necessity of a hypothesis being empirically *testable*. It is when we figure out the implications of a hypothesis in place and run those out, and then experimentally test to see whether those implications are fulfilled or not. That is where the empirical connection happens, and there the empirical connection can be readily at hand for those who have the conceptual equipment in place to see it.

It is still not foolproof. Let me illustrate this. Back in the early 1940s, the United States was at war with the Axis Powers, and unbeknown to most of the population of the United States, research had begun at Oak Ridge in Tennessee, and in Chicago, and at other locations. Research had begun to possibly develop atomic weapons. The theories had been spun out. Einstein had sought an audience with Roosevelt. Funding had been found, and research was proceeding. There are two little stories in that context, and let me start with one at the end. When we dropped the dreadful atomic weapons on Hiroshima and Nagasaki, we honestly did not know whether they were going to work or not. We did not have enough of them to have run a test. And so, here was a case where there was confirmation of the hypothesis with very high stakes and at the last minute in the game. Earlier on, because we were working in such an area of darkness, out at the University of Chicago in a lab that had been constructed in the bowels of an old building, the scientists were trying to get some kind of experimental confirmation about critical mass because they were working with the notion that in order to get a sustained atomic reaction, you were going to have to have a critical mass of the necessary material in the same place at the same time. And it was very important to find out what that critical mass was, and how that was going to work. A lot of hypotheses got spun.

But it was all head-work until those hypotheses got tested experimentally, and the testing was tragically humorous. What the guys did was take a big pool table left over from recreational facilities at the university, and they put lumps of radioactive material on the slate bed of the pool table. I do not know what element they were working with. It was probably uranium, or plutonium, or one of those dreadful things. Then, two scientists with a pull-bridge, you know that thing with a little bumpy end on it that you use to steady your cue stick, gently pushed those piles of material closer to one another from opposite ends of the table. They did this with lots of Geiger counters set up, growing progressively madder and madder as the things approached. Then, if it got too hot, they could pull them apart a little bit. Well, they confirmed what they were looking for about what the right amount was needed in all of that. The tragic side of it is that within a relatively short period of time, several years, most of the people who were involved in that experiment died of radiation sickness. There were other consequences that they had not thought through with the attention and the care that they had needed in order to take the precautions that they needed to take.

Even in the 1940s, anyone knew perfectly well that if they were working with x-rays, they needed to have shielding. Back in the 1920s and 1930s, there were many individuals who worked with x-rays. Dentists, shoe-store clerks, and other people did not take the necessities of shielding into account, and they paid a bitter price. What is my point? My point is that all of the theoretical apparatus about atomic energy pays out with reading on Geiger counters, with radiation sickness, with bombs that work. There is the empirical connection at the tag end. This kind of empirical connection is called *conformational empiricism*. The empirical link is made at the level of confirmation rather than at the level of source. And, of course, that is exactly what was going on with all of the experimentation about atomic power, and all of that output certainly was observable.

Notice, of course, that you cannot do this kind of thing without having a hypothesis in place. It would not have occurred to anyone to put large amounts of radioactive material in one place and then, perhaps, rig an explosive device that would implode it together in a chief critical mass. Unless someone already had the idea of the possibility of sustainable atomic reactions, and the idea contra to many eons of scientific traditions about the law of the conservation of matter, had not someone had the idea that matter and energy were in some way interchangeable, and then articulated that out in a theory that could be put to work? So there had to be a hypothesis in place. You cannot test what you have not hypothesized. But the fact that there has to be a hypothesis in place says absolutely *nothing* about where that hypothesis comes from.

Now, there is an interesting question there. And quite frankly, the interesting thing about that interesting question is, I think, that to a large extent, we do not know where the insights that a creative genius will produce come from. But call it inspiration if you would like. Call it the lucky byproduct of someone whose head is wired just a little bit differently from the rest of us. Call it genius. Call it what you will. It is at that point that a contribution gets made, and, quite frankly, there are relatively few of those. Most of us spend our time working out the implications of those insights, testing them, modifying them, working with them, exploring in terms of them, and we are eternally indebted to the Newtons, and the Semmelweises, and all of the others who suddenly ask, "What if we tried it this way?"

Let me also add that not only can you not run the testing and make the progress unless you have a hypothesis in place, it takes more than that. You are going to have to have the apparatus. You are going to have to have the mathematics. We have talked about this before; I am just underscoring it. The apparatus has got to be in place. The mathematics is going to have to be in place. There are going to have to be very creative, what are called "bridging," hypotheses in place that are going to link some grand and dramatic notion, like energy equals mass times the speed of light squared. That links that over to more mundane and macro-level observable things. And so there is a whole apparatus that comes with the enterprise. It is not just a flash of insight, and then suddenly we have consumer products on the one hand, or atomic bombs on the other. Ninety-nine percent of the scientific work, I think, comes in between the insight and the output.

Now, there are possible problems that arise in the context of this kind of *confirmationally* empirical inquiry. With our hypothesis in-hand, one problem is going to be trying to decide between rival hypotheses. There is more than one model of what the structure of the atom might be like. Now, I grew up on the planetary model, and so I visualize the electrons circulating around that nucleus, just sort of like a little solar system. There is a sort of suet pudding model in which the various things sort of look like raisins stuck in a glob of oatmeal. There are lots of different models, different hypotheses, about what atomic structure amounts to. Which route shall we take? Which rival hypothesis shall we pick? Let me illustrate that at a much more obvious level, where the decision is easier to make for most of us. I read years ago, and I have looked for it to try and find it again; maybe my memory is playing tricks on me, but I think I read this, I know I read this.

A wonderful guy, I believe he lived in Florida, had come up with a brilliant hypothesis. He was worried about whether the earth is flat or not. He had decided against the flat earth people that, no, it is not flat, but he came up with a brilliant hypothesis: that the earth is a hollow ball, and that we live on the inside of it. So that when we point up, we are pointing toward the middle of that hollow ball. The entire universe that we observe in the starry heavens is packed into that cavity. It is a sort of interesting and intriguing idea, and one of the things that is intriguing about it is to see how far you can go with it. This brings up the matter of related hypotheses again. You can go pretty far with it as a matter of fact.

One of the problems that you have is that you have an awful lot of universe to pack into the dimensions of something that we know pretty well what size it is. And so one of the things that comes with this particular hypothesis about the structure of the world is that the closer things get to the middle, the more and more they shrink. So they get tiny as they get toward the middle. Functionally, there is an infinite amount of space relative to the size of the object, even though actually the amount of space available is finite. Well, how far do you want to go with that? How far do you want to go in being patient with those dear members of the Flat Earth Society, which is still alive and well? Those dear members of the Flat Earth Society want to say that the earth, indeed, is flat. One can maintain that, and one can maintain it even in the face of very substantial counterevidence.

Standard evidence for the curvature of the earth is what happens when a sailing ship goes over the horizon. And as a sailing ship goes over the horizon, the hull disappears first, and then the mast, and then the sails, and then the little pendant on top because the curvature of the earth's surface interposes itself between us and the ship we are looking at—and that is something that one can readily observe. It is a very strong confirmation of the claim that the surface of the earth is curved. It is strong confirmation for the claim that the surface of the earth is curved as long as light travels in straight lines. But on the other hand, if light travels in curved lines, then the earth could be flat, and the line of sight could be curved, and we would get the same phenomenon. Now trust me, you know there is no reason to think that the earth is flat, but it is an interesting question. How far does one go in weighing alternative hypothetical explanations, and how does one decide?

That is where matters that we discussed back in Lecture Nine come into play. That is where matters like the scope, and the fertility, and the capacity for self correction, and the way this theory meshes with other theories in use, and the breadth of data that this theory will cover, all come into play. Whether this theory generates experimental situations that put it to the test and help us improve it, fine-tune it, and make it better, as compared to other theories. The decision procedure, then, between alternative hypotheses is typically a pragmatic decision procedure. It is going to be a decision procedure that works in terms of the quality and reliability of the output that comes out of the theory, and the productivity characteristics of the theory as compared to its rivals.

Now, I would invite you, just as an exercise, to—in your mind—consider the source that I referred to last time, von Daniken and his book *Chariots of the Gods*. Consider the hypotheses that are offered there to explain the pyramids in the Yucatan, and so on, to other alternative hypotheses, and see how the pragmatics of it works out. And, of course, remember along the way that you are not only looking for scope, and mesh, and consistency, and self-correctedness, and all of those Lecture Nine items that we talked about, but that we are also keeping Ockham's Razor firmly in-hand so that we do not hypothesize any more than we absolutely have to.

There is another problem though, not just a problem of choosing between rival hypotheses—that is a nice problem. Sometimes the problem is coming up with a hypothesis all together. We have data that we just do not understand. It does not make sense to us. And we scratch our heads and, perhaps in a quandary, try to figure out how we can get a handle on the phenomenon here—and this does not have to be at some high, exotic, abstract, scientific level. This could be a police detective at work, and the police detective discovers that the stolen car has a hundred miles more on its odometer than it should have—and that is a fact that he has got to take into account. He is going to have to come up with an explanatory hypothesis that will explain why the odometer has the extra hundred miles.

Here is, perhaps, a rather dimwitted husband who notices quite regularly that whenever the phone rings and he answers it, whoever it is on the other end hangs up—and this puzzles him. He wonders why in the world does whoever is calling hang up when he answers the phone. Maybe he will eventually hypothesize that one particular person is calling again and again, and that that person does not want to talk to him, and consequently that is why the hanging up is occurring. But that is a hypothesis that may not be on our dense husband's radar screen. It may take a flash of insight on his part to think something is going on.

Okay, in this view, the pedigree of a hypothesis is of far less importance than the tradition had held. Einstein was one of the major players at the working level in breaking the hold of genetic empiricism on the scientific enterprise, and insisting that conformational empiricism was the proper name of the game. Einstein himself generated ideas right and left. I wish I had time to tell you a long story, but I will tell you a very short story about Albert Einstein. I never knew the gentlemen, but I knew some people who did know him. They told me that in his house at the institute in Princeton, he had little pads of paper, little three-by-five notepads, hole punched in the corner, string-tied. On the other end of the string, a pencil stub was tied on. These hung over nails, literally, throughout his house—in the kitchen, on both sides of his bed, in the living room, next to the TV set, in the bathroom next to the john. There were these little pads of paper and pencils within reach because the man had ideas. He wanted to be able to write those ideas down when he had them, no matter what he was doing. And so, wherever he was, whatever he was doing, when he had a flash, he would grab that pad, and he would scribble down on it, and then hang it back on the nail, and then go on about his business.

The wonderful part of the story I have told is that about once every week or so, he would methodically go through the house and gather up all of those pads. He would tear off the sheets that had been written on, collate them, sit down in his chair, and turn on his good light. He would go through those slips of paper—one at a time—reading them over, "seeing [and I am quoting] if any of them made sense." And I am told that maybe one out of 20 did, and the others got wadded up and thrown away. I cannot illustrate more vividly that science, the empiricism of science, is not in its source—it is in the work that we can do with it.

Lecture Eighteen
Hypotheses and Experiments—A Closer Look

Scope:

There are at least two epistemic uses for experiments. Some are aimed at *discovering* patterns and relationships that will help generate descriptive and explanatory knowledge. Others are aimed at *testing* the theories or ideas that we entertain so as to *confirm* (not prove) or *disconfirm* them. In either situation, methodological considerations are of supreme importance. These include the identification and control of variables, the interpretation of experimental output, replicability, and the reliability of sampling techniques.

Outline

I. Experiments may take place in laboratories and in the field. They may be contrived or involve only the detailed examination of existing data. However structured and carried out, there are at least two uses for experiments that are of interest to modern rational empiricists.

   A. Some are aimed at *discovering* patterns and relationships that will help generate descriptive and explanatory knowledge.

   Example: Running experiments to discover the impact of various chemical compounds on a variety of infectious organisms and on the plants and animals they infect.

   B. Others are aimed at *testing* the theories or ideas that we entertain so as to *confirm* (not prove) or *disconfirm* them.

   Example: Running experiments to see whether or not objects of different mass actually accelerate at the same rate in free fall as theory predicts.

II. In either kind of use, methodological considerations are of supreme importance if we are concerned at all to think our way to a reliable conclusion. These considerations must include such things as the identification and control of variables and the reliability of sampling techniques.

   A. Identifying relevant variables is not easy.

1. What factors do we need to take into account when trying to decide whether or not a particular alternative therapy for a particular degenerative disease is, in fact, therapeutic?
    a. Many factors may be relevant, and some may not be obvious.
    b. Consider, for instance, whether or not the particular disease is in any way cyclical. Malaria, for example, is one of many diseases in which there is a regular variation between more intense and less intense symptoms.
2. In addition to all the characteristics of a procedure under investigation and all the characteristics of the contexts in which it is being assessed, we must also take into account all the *limiting conditions* that may apply in the case at hand.
    a. Prejudice, bias, faulty instrumentation, lack of due care, and the like are always possible. The alleged achievement of "cold fusion" in 1989 was very likely flawed by contaminated equipment.
    b. Such things are relevant because they affect outcomes.
    c. Their presence, however, can be very difficult to see. That's why repeatability, public access, publication in scientific journals, and the like are needed when we want the results of our work to be reliable.
B. Controlling relevant variables can be very difficult, particularly when working with human subjects.
    1. It is very difficult to get humans to honestly report the results of experimentation.
    2. There is also a general problem with volunteered information. Consider, for example, the data in the Kinsey Reports on sexual behavior. People who volunteer to talk about their sex lives may or may not be like everyone else in the kind of sex lives they lead.
    3. When relevant variables are controlled, experimental results should be replicable.

    Negative example: As already noted, the widely publicized production of "cold fusion" in 1989 was not replicable, and it was widely thought at the time that this was because crucial variables had not been controlled in the lab where it was claimed to have occurred. This is why reputable researchers publish the details of their experiments, not just their results.

C. The reliability of the sampling techniques used in gathering data is crucial.

Example: It may be quite important to find out such things as whether a political poll was taken by telephone: People who have telephones and people who do not have telephones probably differ in terms of their economic status and their political outlook.

Essential Reading:

Darrell Huff, *How to Lie with Statistics*.

Recommended Reading:

Joel Best, *Damned Lies and Statistics*.

Questions to Consider:

1. The Kinsey Report (a study of human sexual behavior) was widely criticized when it was published because the people included in the study volunteered to participate. Why might one think that this was a relevant criticism?

2. If the proof of the pudding is in the eating, why isn't the proof of a hypothesis in the experimental results? Why doesn't the fact that a cancer went away *prove* that the therapy employed on the patient (Laetril, Krebiozin, or something similar) was "right" (that is, the source of the cure)?

Lecture Eighteen
Hypotheses and Experiments—A Closer Look

In our last two sessions, we have been talking about the crucial role that hypothesis construction plays in the building of our understanding of what is going on around us. We looked at whether the understanding that we are seeking is broad, and abstract, and scientific in some very complex sense, or whether it is everyday, ordinary matters that we are trying to understand and bring within the scope of being able to deal with them and work through them. One of the important points that I have been trying to make, especially at our last session, was that the hypothetical constructions that are used when we build our explanations and our understanding of what is going on around us have empirical connections. But the empirical connections do not necessarily come from their source. Those empirical connections often have to do with how the hypothesis is *confirmed*—how it is tested out.

And that brings us to the other side of what is really one package of issues. And that is to say that we cannot talk about the role of hypothesis in understanding what is going on around us if we do not talk about the role of experimentation, which is what we use to *confirm* or *disconfirm* the hypothesis that we are working with. Hypothesis and experimentation ride together, with the hypothesis furnishing us with the broad frame of reference in terms of which we are trying to build an understanding, and the experimentation checking to see whether or not the implications of that hypothesis pay out at the end.

Now, experimentation comes in many forms. It can be used for many reasons. I have very fond memories from my childhood, and maybe some of you have similar memories from your own childhood. But I remember one particular Christmas when the big Christmas present from Mom and Dad was a genuine Gilbert Hall of Science Chemistry Set, and I had wanted a genuine Gilbert Hall of Science—I didn't want any Porter Ken lab—I wanted a genuine Gilbert Hall of Science Chemistry Set. I was so thrilled. Now it may be good fortune that I never blew up the house, or it may be foresight on the part of the good people at the Gilbert Hall of Science in not putting anything in that rig that was particularly dangerous. But I tried everything that my childish imagination could think of in the name of experimenting. I experimented morning, noon, and night. I did not have any hypothesis in-hand. I was not trying to confirm some insight that I had tentatively put forward to understand this, or that, or the other. I just wanted to see what would happen if I put some of this with some of that, and shook it up real hard.

Actually, there is nothing wrong with that. There is nothing at all wrong with trying different experimental routines just to find out what sort of results you might get. A little bit later on in this session, we will talk about the role that accidents can play at just that point, but I will come back to that. While there is nothing wrong with that chemistry set kind of experimentation, and it might even occasionally come up with something productive or useful, it is much more important to see the central role of experimentation, which is joined at the hip with hypothesis construction. It is experimentation that is designed to confirm or deny some hypothesis that is in place, and that can be a very important enterprise. I am thinking particularly today in the context of the testing that we do to determine the efficacy and the safety of pharmaceuticals, and this is not just some random thing. I do not think the lab scientists that are working at all of the different pharmaceutical companies are just tossing various things together, and shaking them up real hard, and seeing what happens. There is medical research that has gone on that has, perhaps, put some illumination into an area of a particular disease and has suggested some possibility of a therapeutic technique. There is, after all, all of the history going back into the 19th century, but amazingly only going back into the 19th century— all of the history of the development of pharmaceuticals, and antibiotics, and vaccines, and all of the rest of those things that we rely upon every day of our lives to keep us alive. But with the hypothesis in place that a particular mold, let's say, is going to be discouraging for the propagation of certain microbes, we are going to want to run tests on that and see if it reliably works.

That is going to be one phase of our experimentation. We are also going to want to run tests on the side effects of injecting that mold into some critter because it would not be very helpful if the injection perhaps cured a case of pneumonia, but caused instant and horrible death because of some kind of toxic impact of the mold itself. So, with the hypothesis that this may be effective, we go into very extensive controlled experimental settings, usually starting with lab animals and working our way gradually in the way of human testing in order to demonstrate—because the FDA says we have to—not only that the drug is effective, but also that it is safe. If we did not have some hypothesis in place to begin with, the stumbling upon an effective and safe therapy would be simply good luck. The rigorous research programs that are established by the pharmaceutical companies show that under the governing ages of hypothesis and predictions, a research program can be set up that is productive in the long run. Pharmaceuticals can be produced that are effective and are safe. So, hypothesis construction and experimentation are working hand-in-glove, working together to a common end.

Now, whether we are just putting stuff together and shaking it up to see what happens on the one hand, or whether we are engaged in a very systematic research program on the other, methodological considerations are going to be of supreme importance if we are going to get any kind of reliable results out of the experimental testing that we are doing. We want to think that the results are going to be enduring, are going to be the same under somewhat varying circumstances to the extent, then, that I am thinking of it from the very commercial standpoint. We think to the extent that we could market this product and stake the reputation, the fortune, and the future of the company on it—to say nothing of the fortune and the future of the people who use the product that we are selling to them. There is a whole lot at stake here, and methodological considerations in the experimental program are going to be of supreme importance to guarantee the reliability of that output. These considerations involve identifying a number of things. For one thing, they involve identifying to the extent that we can control and identify the variables that are in play in the situation that we are dealing with. Go back to our example of the chilling effect of a mold culture on streptococcus. There are so many different things that could have an impact on the efficacy of what, ultimately, turns out to be penicillin. Whether or not it works is going to depend upon the medium in which the mold culture has been grown. It is going to depend upon the virulence of the streptococcus bacteria that is being introduced. It may depend upon the conditions in the laboratory: the temperature, the humidity, the kind of light that is at play.

Now, I do not imagine any laboratory is going to be running serious experiments under high-intensity ultraviolet light unless they are aware of the fact that they are doing so, because you certainly would not want to market a product as being a very effective germ killer, only to discover after the fact that the reason all of the germs were dying was because of UV radiation in the lab where you did the experimentation. So you have got to identify a host of different things that are involved, and you have got to, as they say, control for them. And one of the interesting things about the experimental process is going to be controlling different variables at different times to see what the effects are if we change this one, holding these constant, or if we change these, holding this in constant, working our way through systematically and methodically to see what kind of output we get. So, we have got to identify the relevant variables.

That is not easy. How do we decide which variables are going to be relevant in a particular case? What is crucial in determining whether this therapeutic technique is effective or not? I heard a very interesting story just last summer at a conference out on the West Coast. We were talking about alternative medicines, and we were talking about the interesting fact that with almost any alternative medical, therapeutic technique that someone might suggest there is going to be a wagonload of anecdotal evidence out there to support the claim that this therapy works. Sometimes, one of the problems with alternative medical techniques is that they have not been subjected to rigorous, controlled verification. The only evidence we have is anecdotal. I took it, I feel better. And to the layman, and that includes me—I took it, and I feel better—that sounds pretty good. Well, the point of the presentation that I was listening to was focusing in on one particular interesting phenomenon.

Let me share it with you because it helps make the point very nicely. Many serious human illnesses are significantly "cyclical" in their pattern. Malaria is one particular good example, where there is a regular variation of intensification of symptoms, sloping off of symptoms, intensification of symptoms, and so on. But it is only one of many diseases and conditions that are, to a significant extent, cyclical in their pattern. Add that to an interesting characteristic of human beings. And I believe this to be true. I certainly know that it is true of me. I do not like going to the doctor, and so, typically, I am going to put off going to the doctor until I feel really bad. Then, grudgingly, I will go, and grudgingly I may even tell him the truth, or I may keep some secrets because I do not want him to tell me things I do not want to hear. I am very human that way. So, grudgingly, I go into the doctor's office. I get examined, and the doctor tells me to take two aspirins and call him in the morning, or whatever he tells me to do, and I get better. The point is that if the condition that I have is cyclical, and like most people I wait until I am at the absolute troth of the cycle before I break down and go to the doctor, then it probably does not matter a whole lot what the doctor says or does not say, or does or does not do, I am going to be feeling better not too long after that visit as the cycle comes around.

And so he might give me some medicine that is in fact efficacious for my condition. He might wave a wand over me and say "Be well." He might say that I need to meditate more. He might say that I have got to increase the bran content in my diet. And whatever he has said, I go home. I very industriously meditate, wave a wand over my head, eat lots of bran, and I feel better, and I write testimony. Now, do not misunderstand me. I do not mean to suggest for a moment that every alternative therapeutic technique that has ever been suggested is no more than a kind of accident, that the benefits that come with it are kind of an accidental byproduct of regular patterns of cyclical diseases—that is certainly not the case.

What I do want to suggest is that in the area of medicine, perhaps more so than in any other area, because so much is immediately at stake in the area of medicine, we really want to know whether the therapeutic technique that is suggested to us and that we are being urged to take has been checked out and proven to be safe and effective. That is why we have the Food and Drug Administration. Unfortunately, human nature being what it is, and human wishful thinking being what it is, there are those among us who do not pay any particular attention to the careful work of the FDA and will go harrying off all over the globe for Prothiazine or Laetrile, or apricot pits, or whatever is the latest guru's suggestion as a proper way to deal with whatever dread condition that we have, which is tragically sad. And I am sticking with this for just a moment. The reason that it is sad is because a person who gets caught up in that kind of irresponsible and untested medical play probably is not going to be availing himself or herself of techniques and resources that are available that might do them some good.

It is very difficult to discover the relevant factors. There may be factors that are in play that would not cross our minds. That is why I brought up the cyclical nature of diseases, because that is a factor that had never occurred to me before I heard the presentation that I have been telling you about. But the medical researcher has got to try to figure out, as best as he or she can, what all the different variables are that might be in play, and then try to control those in such a way as to reach some kind of reliable conclusion.

In addition to all of the characteristics of the procedure that we are trying out, and all of the characteristics of the condition that we are trying to deal with, and all of the characteristics of the context in which we are working, there are also things that we need to take into account in every experimental situation, things that we have already talked about—so I really only need to remind you. It is the possible invasion of "limiting conditions" that are going to interfere with the reliability of the data collection that we are doing, and those limiting conditions could be as simple as dirty glassware. They could be as complicated as prejudice or bias on the part of the person who is doing the research. And all of those vulnerabilities that go with the fact that the inquiry is being done by finite human beings are going to be there, and we are going to have to try to control for them.

So we are not just trying to control and get standard temperature and pressure, and we are not just trying to control in terms of what the known characteristics of the disease in question are. But we are also trying to control in terms of our own understanding of our biases and our prejudices in terms of the due care that we recognize must be given to research of this kind—which sometimes, out of laziness, we do not give. If we can get those limiting conditions under control, along with controlling all the variables that are in play, then the probability of reliable results to our hypothesis testing, the probability of that reliability is going to rise very significantly.

Back in 1989, I believe, you probably read, as I did, the announcement in the paper that "cold fusion" had been achieved out in the Southwest. Wow! What a breakthrough—nuclear fusion in a test tube, at room temperature. Talk about solving the energy problems of the globe, would that it had worked. But all kinds of limiting conditions got into play. Little footnote: One of the reasons why a lot of people were very suspicious in that instance, of the reliability of what was being reported, was that there was a great rush. There was a great haste to announce the results in the media before the reports of the lab work had been published in the scientific journals. And why do you suppose scientists publish their lab work in the journals? And that gets back to repeatability. That gets back to public access. That gets back to, once again, all of those things that we know perfectly well we need to keep track of when we want the results of our work to be reliable. But in the haste and the passion of a flash of insight or a laboratory accident, we are just likely to forget the relevance of all of these things simply because they affect outcome. All of them are difficult simply because they are sometimes hard to see.

A couple of other examples can help explain some of the things that are going on here too. Do you remember when Pepsi-Cola was running a taste test? You had to pass the Pepsi challenge, and people were offered glasses of Pepsi and glasses of Coca-Cola, and, I think, RC Cola, and so on. The claim was that blindfolded people could pick out the one that tasted best, and that an alarmingly high percentage of the time, the one that blindfolded people picked out turned out to be Pepsi. So, anybody who said that they were a Coca-Cola fanatic, or an RC Cola fanatic, was challenged to face the Pepsi challenge. I do not know how scientifically that particular test was run, but I did notice that whenever they would have pictures of this in the TV ads and the newspapers, the people who were facing the Pepsi challenge either were wearing blindfolds, or the colas were in opaque cups that were not marked with brand names or anything of the sort. Why is that? Because, of course, our anticipation and our identification of a product. If we have positive feelings about that product, they can very much affect the way the product tastes to us.

I played a cruel trick one time on a colleague of mine who was, I will be bold here, a wine snob, an insufferable wine snob, but he was a dear friend anyway. And in an antique shop, I came upon an old earthenware sherry bottle that dated from who knows how long ago. It was very antiquated, and it had cobwebs, and it really looked authentic. It probably had been made in a factory 30 miles up the road in Mechanicsville the day before, but it looked good to my eye. What I did was, I washed out the inside of that old sherry bottle, and I filled it with the cheapest jug sherry that I could buy at the drugstore. It was Gallo, or Pisano, or something of the sort—perfectly good drinking sherry, nothing wrong with those brands at all. But I filled this old jug with it, and I took it to a wine-tasting party where I knew my friend was going to be. He simply went gaga over the nuances, the subtle—I will not bore you with the story, but the point, of course, was that all of his prejudices, all of his mindset, were there thinking that this was an ancient and discovered bottle of sherry. It was wonderful. If I had set out the jug and poured it for him in a Dixie cup, I do not think I would have gotten the same response at all.

Controlling variables can be very difficult, particularly if we are working with human subjects, and I will spend the last few minutes that I have dealing with that phase of it. Human beings themselves are hard to control. It is very difficult to get humans to honestly report the results of experimentation that is being done. You may be old enough to remember, and this goes way back, the Kinsey Reports on sexual behavior in the human male and sexual behavior in the human female, which was an electrifying set of data when it was published at mid-century. One of the big problems about that was that all of the information on which the reports were based was self-reported information coming from people who volunteered to be interviewed for a report on sexual behaviors. Now, it may be that people who like to talk about their sex life are no different from everybody else in the kind of sex life they live. Then again, it may be that people with, shall I say, particularly dramatic or colorful sex lives may like to talk about it more than people whose sexual activities are more pedestrian and more ordinary. There is a human factor in self-reported data that makes that kind of data highly suspect, and this is just one of those areas in which when the experimentation that is being done involves human beings—what they do, and what they say about what they do. Extra caution absolutely has to be taken.

Among those extra cautions that we need to take is looking for replicability, especially in the case of humans again. Can we run the same test, time after time after time, and get some kind of consistent results? If the results are not replicable then the hypothesis is in severe jeopardy. Now, this is not just in the case of psychological studies and things that involve humans. Going back to cold fusion again when the dead giveaway that the cold fusion experiment was not what it had been said to be, this is also when the lab reports were published, and every other lab in the country tried to replicate it. No one could get the same results. No one could come within a country mile of the same results, and so everybody said that there has to be a variable that was not identified. There has to be something that made this result happen there that is preventing it from happening here, and then you go to work to figure out what that is. But if replicability is not available, then every danger signal in the world goes up.

Last in the context of humans, and I am out of time, regarding the sampling that you do, it needs to be a random sample, you know that. But the technique that you use in finding your sample is crucially important. In my part of the world, the newspaper regularly publishes polls that are supposed to be very significant relative to the voting preferences of the population at large, and they publish these polls quite regularly as we are ramping up on an election date. Are they trying to influence the vote? I do not know. But there is a very interesting question. How are polls taken? Ah hah! The polls are taken by telephone. Now, is there a statistical difference between people who have telephones and people who do not have telephones in terms of their economic status and their political outlook? You bet there is. And that is why telephone polls are not effective in that kind of experimentation, and that is exactly the kind of thing that we have to watch out for.

Lecture Nineteen
"Normal Science" at Mid-Century

Scope:

Although the paradigm-shifting ideas of Albert Einstein and Werner Heisenberg had already called the "neatness" of modern science into question, in the middle of the 20th century, a stable view of "normal science" was almost universal in the West. This vision was rooted in logical empiricism, with contributions by logicians, mathematicians, scientists, and philosophers. It affirmed the empirical status of scientific descriptions and explanations, establishing "confirmational" empiricism as orthodox and giving free rein to the use of testable hypotheses regardless of their sources. It also insisted that mathematics and logic are purely formal affairs, closing the door on any notion of "synthetic *a priori*" truths. This view has its problems, however; as we will see in Lecture Twenty-Three, it is now severely questioned by both "Postmodern" and "New Age" critics.

Outline

I. Although the paradigm-shifting ideas of Albert Einstein and Werner Heisenberg were already calling the "neatness" of modern rational science into question, in the middle of the 20th century, a stable view of "normal science" was almost universal in the West.

II. This vision was rooted in *logical positivism* (also known by the names *logical empiricism* and the *unity of science movement*), with contributions by logicians, mathematicians, scientists, and philosophers.

  A. Logical positivism amounted to a program with three aims:
   1. The demonstration of the "unity" of all scientific inquiry—an essentially reductionist enterprise;
   2. The separation of scientific discourse from every other kind of discourse in terms of logical and empirical principles; and

      3. The demonstration that all actual or potential knowledge claims (cognitively meaningful claims) fall on the "scientific" side of that divide.

B. Logical positivism was historically connected to Comte's 19th-century positivism, British empiricism, and ultimately, to an Aristotelian (rather than a Platonic) philosophical tradition.

C. It is "logical" in that its criterion for cognitively meaningful discourse makes provision for mathematical and logical claims to be true or false only insofar as they satisfy (or fail to satisfy) purely *formal* standards.

D. It is "empirical" in that its criterion for cognitively meaningful discourse makes provision for descriptive and explanatory claims to be true or false only insofar as they satisfy (or fail to satisfy) purely *experiential* tests.

E. It rules a number of things out of the arena of cognitively meaningful discourse, such as ethics, esthetics, metaphysics, and any and all other enterprises that (by its lights) cannot be "reduced to" natural science.

F. The positivistic side of this vision fixed the empirical status of science in terms of empirical "verification" or "falsification" (depending on who you read). After considerable debate, it established *confirmationally* empirical theories as orthodox, rejected any exalted status for *genetically* empirical theories, and gave free rein to the use of testable hypotheses regardless of their sources.

G. The logical side of this vision insisted that mathematics and logic are purely formal affairs (their claims are necessarily true but empirically empty). This firmly closed the door on any notion of "synthetic *a priori*" truths.

III. This program has its problems, however. Here are five of them:

    A. Reductionism was difficult, if not impossible, to demonstrate.

      1. It is easy to say that psychology and economics have the same theoretical and methodological foundations as physics and chemistry.

      2. It is not so easy to show that this is true, as the ragged history of behavioral psychology demonstrates. George

Lundberg, a famous or infamous behavioral psychologist of the 20th century, once compared a leaf being blown down the street to a man fleeing an angry lynch mob; the only difference between them, he said, was the complexity of the vectors.

B. The exclusion of ethics, religion, and the like from the arena of actual or potential knowledge seems arbitrary and self-defeating. It is one thing to say that evaluative discourse is "cognitively empty" because its claims are not empirically testable. It is difficult if not impossible to show, however, that this claim is, itself, empirically testable in any way.

C. Another, even deeper, problem is that positivism's central commitment to empirical verifiability is itself not open to empirical testing and verification or falsification.
  1. On the other hand, why would we ever expect a rule or a principle to satisfy itself?
  2. As Wittgenstein might point out, although you follow the rules of bridge when playing bridge, the rules of bridge do not *themselves* follow the rules of bridge at all.

D. The program seems committed to a particular conception of how science itself actually works—gradual cumulative progress, governed by a fully rational decision procedure. The actual history of science, however, is thought by many to reveal a different story—one of revolutions and paradigm shifts, governed by the cultures in which it is practiced.

E. There is also widespread mistrust of the scientific enterprise itself as being, perhaps, driven by a program, an ideology, a style, a platform, or a manifesto—in short, not being objective and value-free in the way that it had always claimed itself to be.

IV. As we will see in Lecture Twenty-Three, the program has been severely questioned, along these and other lines, by both "Postmodern" and "New Age" critics. But first we shall look at the logical tools that are at its disposal.

Essential Reading:

Carl Hempel, "Problems and Changes in the Empiricist Criterion of Meaning."

Recommended Reading:

A. J. Ayer, *Language, Truth and Logic.*

Questions to Consider:

1. Why should the NIH privilege Western scientific medicine and marginalize traditional non-Western therapeutic practices? Is this just regional chauvinism, or does it have some real and objective bases?

2. Why should we be nervous about Freud's "unconscious" unless we are equally nervous about muons, black holes, and strings?

Lecture Nineteen
"Normal Science" at Mid-Century

It is only fair to say that at mid-20th century, there was trouble in the domain of "scientific" rational empirical inquiry. Einstein with his theories of relatively, and Heisenberg with his notions of indeterminacy, had already severely called into question some of the orthodoxies of the Newtonian worldview. You will remember that that Newtonian worldview was that everything amounted to matter in motion. Everything could be understood and described, and—with an adequate understanding of natural laws—could be predicted and controlled. Everything was nice, and neat, and well ordered—strictly determinant and intelligible. Principles that are the heart of that Newtonian worldview are by mid-20th century being called into serious question. Is the world strictly determinant at the micro level as well as at the macro level? Heisenberg is saying no. Einstein is not quite sure whether to agree with Heisenberg on that or not.

Another dimension of rational empiricism at that point in history, which in this lecture I am calling "normal science" with scare clips around it, was the notion that rational empirical inquiry was totally objective, substantially value-free, not ideologically driven in any kind of way or fashion, and consequently was naturally and inexorably progressive. It was a smoothly and regularly expanding understanding of a stable and well-ordered natural world. It was not many years at all after mid-century that Thomas Kuhn published a rather disturbing little book called *The Structure of Scientific Revolutions,* which called into question not just the determinateness of the Newtonian worldview and the inviolability and indestructibility of matter in the Newtonian worldview—Einstein and Heisenberg were taking care of that phase of things. Kuhn called into question the very objectivity of the scientific enterprise itself, and—as we shall see in Lecture Twenty-Three—those who have followed Kuhn and what I will be then calling the "post-modern" era have severely called normal science up for review. But what I want to do today is to get as clear an image as we can of what normal science amounted to at mid-century, because in terms of that we can better understand the changes that have taken place in the 50-plus years that have passed since then.

Normal science at mid-20th-century was rooted in a philosophical view that has been known by a variety of labels. "Logical empiricism," "logical positivism," and "The Unity of Science Movement" are three of the labels by which that movement has been called over the years. The men who started this business called themselves the "Vienna Circle," the "Wiener Kreis," and it was a bunch of scientists, engineers, logicians, mathematicians, and others working in and around the university in Vienna. The name that has stuck more solidly than any of the other names is logical positivism, so that is the label that I will use as I refer to them a number of times in this lecture.

Logical positivism amounted to a program, and that program had three main aims. First, the Logical positivists wanted to demonstrate the "unity" of all scientific inquiry, and that is an essential reductionist program. What does that amount to? It amounts to the claim that if we dig deeply enough, we will find that the same root scientific principles are behind all scientific inquiry—that the same principles that are visible; let's say in Newtonian physics, matter in motion, quantifiable measurement, determinism, and all the rest; that translates over absolutely and smoothly without loss into any area of genuinely rational empirical scientific inquiry, be that biology, psychology, economics, or maybe even history. So there was a reductionist program to suggest that all of the more specialized and later sciences were essentially part of the same nuclear unit, maybe not as well-developed or mature, but part of the same organic plant.

The second aim, and it is very closely related to the first one, was to separate anything that was bona fide rational empirical scientific inquiry from anything that was not, and to clearly label anything that did not follow the empirical and rational methodology of scientific inquiry, anything that was labeled as beyond the pale. Now, that has some interesting implications that we will turn to momentarily, but let me just flag one of them now. Ever since people have been writing, and studying, and trying to explain what is going on in the world, one area of human error has been ethics—not just what do we do, but what ought we to do. And the clear-cut implication of normal science at mid-century was that science is a value-free enterprise. It has nothing to do with normative dimensions at all, and, consequently, those normative areas of inquiry have nothing to do with knowledge, evidence, demonstration, or truth at all. They belong to some other non-cognitive, non-rational, non-empirical human enterprise—perhaps the emotions, perhaps the will. Science, though, is the good stuff, and that other stuff—as I say—is beyond the pale.

So, the third point looks beyond the "unity" of all scientific inquiry and the separation of genuinely scientific inquiry in terms of its "logical" and "empirical" techniques. The third point, then, is the demonstration that any enterprise that is not logical and empirical in its techniques is on the other side of a great divide from anything that is scientific.

Now this movement has deep historical roots. It also has shallow historical roots. The shallow historical roots go back to the 19th century. A French philosopher, August Comte, the father of French positivism, was a wonderfully interesting character and sort of an intellectual rascal. I enjoy reading August Comte. He said at one point in his life that he suddenly realized that if he was going to continue to make the wonderful progress and understanding for which he was so deservedly famous, that he was simply going to have to stop muddying his mind with reading things that had been written by other authors. He would practice mental hygiene, he said, and confine himself thereafter, to reading only his own writings. Well, there was a positive side to 19th-century positivism as well. The root there is into a hard and fast attempt, an attempt at a hard and fast distinction between what amounts to genuine science, what amounts to myth making, what amounts to metaphysics, and what amounts to speculation, and from Comte's point of view, religion and all of that sort of thing.

There are roots that run deeper back into British empiricism. Locke, Barkley, and Hume are examples. And there are roots that run very deeply, indeed, back to the empirical care with which Aristotle carried out his work in early Greek times. And you will find as you look at the logical positivists, their affinities, then, are to the broad empirical traditions of philosophy. And those empirical traditions in philosophy, in the West at any rate, are clearly part of the Aristotelian legacy, rather than the Platonic legacy that we were talking about at the beginning of this series. Logical positivism is *logical* in that its criterion for significant discourse includes *formal* criteria for logical and mathematical claims. There is no pretense among the logical positivists that logic and math are empirical sciences, that logic and math have been discovered by an examination of observable data. They are quite willing to accept that logic and mathematics are free creations of human intelligence that contingently happen to be useful in manipulating and understanding the world around them, but they are perfectly willing to accept into the fold of legitimate rational empirical inquiry, all of the apparatus of logic and mathematics and all that can be done with it. So they are not just empiricists. They are not just positivists. They are logical positivists.

The empirical side of their enterprise makes clear and distinct provision for descriptive and explanatory claims to be accepted into the body of scientific discourse, only insofar as those claims somehow satisfy some kind of *experiential* tests. Now, notice I said "somehow satisfy some kind of experiential tests." There was argument among the logical positivists themselves over what kind of experiential tests claims would have to pass in order to qualify as genuinely empirical, and how they would have to pass them, but there is going to be an empirical benchmark there of some sort to be passed in some way. It got articulated differently, most regularly in terms of what has been called the "empirical verifiability criterion of meaning." The notion here was quite simply that in order for a claim, an utterance, a piece of discourse, to be scientifically meaningful at all, much less to be true, it had to be open to empirical verification. And if it was not open to empirical verification for one reason or another, then it would be simply placed on the other side of that great abyss, over there with non-science, non-cognition, and I will use their word, "nonsense." Those positivists were tough-minded, or hardheaded.

So it was logical, and it was empirical. And we have just seen as we have been anticipating, but let me underscore it again that because it was logical, and empirical, and would not admit anything that did not satisfy those benchmarks, it relegated a great number of things outside the arena—not just the arena of Science with a capital "S," but outside the arena of knowledge, outside the arena of potential knowledge, outside the arena of sense and over into that arena of non-cognitive, nonsensical discourse. The list is long including ethics, aesthetics, metaphysics, and religion.

Here is what it boils down to. Remember we started out saying it is a reductionist enterprise? And if we have got an enterprise over here that cannot be "reduced to" a state of unity with the core of the scientific enterprise, if that reduction cannot be brought off, then from the positivistic point of view it is simply relegated. It is dismissed.

Well, I think you can see the kind of image of the scientists that would go with this kind of program. They were cold, aloof, and wise almost beyond human measurement, irreligious—just that cold, clear, blue light of science giving us foresight and understanding of facts.

There are some very serious problems that are attached to this, but before I go on to those problems there is one other thing that I want to deal with a little bit more, precisely on what empirical verification amounts to. And let me say in passing that you can get into a nice argument—and the argument has been pursued by dozens of writers—over whether we want to talk about empirical "verification," or whether we want to talk about empirical "falsification." And there are reasons behind the debate that went on between the verifiers and the falsifiers. Karl Popper is the one who taught most about empirical falsification as the benchmark of genuine scientific discourse, in that it was falsifiable, meaning it was open to decisive crucial testing.

There are severe difficulties with any notion of a claim being strictly, definitively verifiable or falsifiable. I am not going to pursue those at any kind of length, but I think you can anticipate and understand some of the shape of the problem here. A very large number of scientific claims are general claims, claims of the general form, all S's are P's. How are you going to definitively verify a universal claim, ever? You cannot. The best you can do on universal claims is some level of probability. Other scientific claims are very particular and individual. This S has this set of properties, or there is an S that has this set of properties. How are we ever going to definitively falsify a claim that is that particular and narrow? The mere fact that we find a thousand different things that do not have these properties does not definitively show that there is not one out there somewhere that we have not looked at yet that does. So there was a great deal of back and forth over do we want verificationism? Do we want falsificationism? Do we want strict verification? Do we want verification in principle? Do we want indirect verification in principle? That is traced out very beautifully in an essay by Carl Hempel called "Problems and Changes in the Empirical Verifiability Criterion of Meaning." It has been reprinted widely and is worth the read if you are interested in this piece of the history of the development of scientific inquiry.

Bottom line on that is that most settle on what A.J. Ayer called indirect verificationism, which, in a nutshell, amounts to this, and it is a beautiful notion, beautiful enough that I want to state it for you: "A claim is properly scientific if it can be directly observationally verified," no problem, "or if it can be indirectly observationally verified." And what does indirect observational verification amount to? It amounts to there being directly verifiable results that can be predicted on the basis of your hypothesis and certain other allied and associated hypotheses that cannot be predicted on the basis of those allied or associated hypotheses by themselves. So, if your hypothesis, along with related and associated hypotheses in place, generates observational data that can be confirmed, that you could not have generated, or foreseen, or predicted, absent the theoretical contribution that you are making, then that theoretical contribution is said to have been indirectly empirically verified. That is a long way from looking through the eyepiece of a microscope and seeing a quantum leap. But since one does not look through the eyepiece of microscopes and see quantum leaps, something like indirect verification has to come into play to make the notion that science is genuinely empirically rooted.

There are problems. Reductionism is easy to announce. All proper science is part of one unified, organic whole. It is much harder to bring it off. An awful lot of energy got spent in the 20th century in the spotty history of behavioral psychology trying to demonstrate that psychology really was logical empirical stuff, just like physics. George Lundberg, a famous or infamous behavioral psychologist of the 20th century, once said, and this is a paraphrase but it is very close to what he said: The only difference between a leaf being blown down the street by the wind and a man fleeing an angry lynch mob is the complexity of the vectors. Well, again, that is easy to say. It is very difficult, however, in the case of the man being chased down the street by the lynch mob, to figure out what those vectors are. For that matter, it is fairly difficult to figure out what they are in the case of the leaf being blown by the wind. But, tradition would have it that there are things going on in the mind of the man fleeing the mob, self-reflection, fear, anxiety, all kinds of internal circuitry at work that maybe are not locked into any predictable closed

Newtonian analysis. Maybe they are inaccessible to any closed Newtonian determinant analysis.

There is that question that I alluded to earlier on about the relationship between even early modern science in Newton's time and the question of human free will. It comes into hard focus when we look at normal science in the mid-20th century, when we are trying to decide whether or not there can be a science of human behavior—whether there can be a scientific understanding of the human organism—and there were those who said yes, and there were those who said no.

Here is a second kind of problem. The exclusion of ethics, and religion, and the like from areas of actual or potential knowledge, writing them off as non-cognitive and nonsensical has seen too many critics to be rather arbitrary. It is one thing to simply say that evaluative discourse, in that it is not open to empirical testing, and settlement do not have any cognitive content. But it's another thing to try to figure out what is going on in that kind of discourse, because on the face of it, that kind of discourse is central and crucial to the human enterprise. So maybe it is not enough, even if the positivists are right, to write it off as non-cognitive. It is not enough to simply dismiss it and leave it. Something more needs to be said.

But there is another and even deeper problem that rides with this, and this one is thorny. Suppose someone says that every cognitively meaningful claim must be either a truth of formal logical mathematical analysis, or a claim that is open at least to indirect empirical verification. Suppose someone says that, that is the positivist's posture in a nutshell. What about that claim? Is that a truth of logic or mathematics? Not by a long shot. Is it itself open to empirical testing and verification or falsification, direct or indirect at any level? Sure does not look like it. So there were many critics of positivism and of normal science as it was understood from this positivistic worldview. There were many critics who said that positivism literally shot itself in the foot when it pronounced its platform, its program, its commitment to empirical verifiability, because it was holding up as its banner and as its central commitment a position that did not pass its own tests.

I think it may be easy to see right there, why the last half of the 20th century—as we have moved into a post-modern era influenced by

Kuhn, Heisenberg, Einstein, and many others—has been a period of considerable upheaval and confusion about what is the status of scientific understanding of things that go on in the world. And as we will see when we return to our examination of post-modern rational empiricism, there is widespread mistrust on the part of many individuals of the scientific enterprise itself as being perhaps driven by a program, an ideology, a style, a platform, or a manifesto, not being objective and value-free in the way that it had always claimed itself to be.

On the other hand, this is the last thought for this session: Why would we ever expect a rule or a principle to satisfy itself? We need to bear in mind the difference between the rules of the game and the play of the game, and I very much have Wittgenstein in mind here. If you are going to play Bridge, you are going to have to follow the rules of Bridge. But the rules of Bridge themselves do not follow the rules of Bridge at all. Maybe what the positivists have given us are the rules of science. If so, maybe they do not need to be self-satisfying.

Lecture Twenty
Modern Logic—Truth Tables

Scope:

Wherever our mathematical apparatus, natural laws, and state descriptions come from, we draw inferences from them according to the canons of logic. By the beginning of the 20th century, logic far surpassed the traditional syllogism. Modern logic still begins with three intuitive (though no longer thought to be *necessarily* true) assumptions about the truth or falsity of indicative sentences, and these are still called the laws of *identity*, *non-contradiction*, and *excluded middle*. These laws are used in constructing truth tables on which basic operators are defined for *negation*, *conjunction*, *disjunction*, and *implication*. These, in turn, provide the tools to determine the truth or falsity of compound sentences of great complexity and to establish rules of inference and standards for validity. Logic also expedites the analysis of sets and switching circuits and the construction of computer languages.

Outline

I. Whether we hypothesize, discover, or create the mathematics, covering laws, and state descriptions that we use in explaining what we observe, we need a reliable apparatus for drawing inferences from them. This is provided by modern logic, an adaptation and extension of the syllogistic logic that we examined in Lectures Four through Seven. We shall examine the rudiments of modern logic in this and the following two lectures, but what we cover here only scratches the surface. You can find a thorough treatment of the history of logic in William and Martha Kneale's *The Development of Logic*.

II. Modern logic is still based on three intuitively attractive (though no longer thought to be *necessarily* true) assumptions about the truth or falsity of indicative sentences; these are usually called the laws of *identity*, *non-contradiction*, and *excluded middle.*

    A. *Identity.* For any adequately explicit, indicative descriptive sentence *p*, if it is true in a given context, it is true throughout that context, and if it is false in a given context, then it is false throughout that context. For example, if "It is raining [here, now]" is true (false) in one line of an argument, it must be true (false) in every line of that argument.

B. *Non-contradiction.* For any adequately explicit, indicative descriptive sentence *p*, if it is true in a given context, then its denial is false in that context, and if it is false in a given context, then its denial is true in that context. For example, if "It is raining [here, now]" is true (false) in one line of an argument, then its denial must be false (true) in every line of that argument.

C. *Excluded middle.* There is no *tertium quid* truth value for any adequately explicit, indicative descriptive sentence *p*. "True" and "false" are the only options available.

III. These principles are intuitively attractive, but they are not necessarily true. They are assumptions, or postulates, for the system. They collectively presume that what adequately explicit, indicative descriptive sentences are about is coherent and consistent.

IV. These laws are utilized in constructing truth tables in terms of which basic logical operators are defined for *negation, conjunction, disjunction, implication,* and *equivalence.*

operation	symbol	read as	meaning of symbol
negation	~	"curl"	it is not the case that
conjunction	•	"dot"	and; but; furthermore; nevertheless
disjunction	∨	"wedge"	or (in an inclusive sense); unless
implication	⊃	"horseshoe"	if...then; implies; causes
equivalence	≡	"triple bar"	are equivalent; if and only if

V. Using ~ for "it is not the case that"; • for such terms as "and," "but," "furthermore," "nevertheless," etc.; ∨ for such terms as "or," "unless," etc.; ⊃ for such terms as "implies," "causes," and "if...then"; and ≡ for such expressions as "are equivalent" and "if and only if," we may define our operators on truth tables as follows:

A. *Negation*: This is simply a graphic representation of the law of non-contradiction.

	Guide Column	Statement			Guide Column		Statement
Negation	p	$\sim p$	Conjunction		p	q	$p \bullet q$
	T	F			T	T	T
	F	T			T	F	F
					F	T	F
					F	F	F

Conjunction: There are contexts in English in which the word *and* not only says that both parts are true but also says something about the sequence in which those events occur. As my mother would have noted, there is all the difference in the world between John and Sue getting married and having a baby, and John and Sue having a baby and getting married. In the logical apparatus, by contrast, the dot does not say anything about sequencing at all. All the dot captures is the claim that both parts are true.

C. *Disjunction*: In some instances in English, when we say p or q, we mean one or the other but not both. That is called *exclusive disjunction* and is relatively rare. There are other occasions when we clearly mean at least one, possibly both. That is called *inclusive disjunction*. The wedge represents inclusive disjunction.

	Guide Column		Statement		Guide Column		Statement
Disjunction	p	q	$p \lor q$	Material Implication	p	q	$p \supset q$
	T	T	T		T	T	T
	T	F	T		T	F	F
	F	T	T		F	T	T

| F | F | F |

| F | F | T |

D. *Material implication*: There are dozens of different expressions in English that amount to something like "if...then." What we want in the logical system is an operator that will represent what all of those different "if...then's" have in common. That leads to what some call the *paradoxes of material implication*. Namely, that "*p* horseshoe *q*" turns out to be true on the third and fourth lines, where *p* itself is false. Still, the common partial meaning of a wide variety of "if...then" expressions is captured rather nicely by the horseshoe—that is, "It is not the case that (*p* and not *q*)," or "*p* does not occur without *q*" (which is what the horseshoe says without suggestion *why* that is the case).

E. The equivalence connector asserts that *p* and *q* have the same truth value. But, as can easily be shown on a larger truth table, it also says that *p* and *q* imply each other (that is, *p* implies *q* and *q* implies *p*).

	Guide Column	Statement
Equivalence	*p* *q*	*p* ≡ *q*
	T T	T
	T F	F
	F T	F
	F F	T

VI. These operators, in turn, provide the tools needed to determine the truth or falsity of compound sentences of great complexity.

    A. Some of these establish basic replacement or substitution rules and rules of inference, as we shall see in Lecture Twenty-One.

    B. Taken together, these rules underwrite a strict test for validity: *An inference is valid if and only if its conclusion can be derived from its premises in a finite number of steps,* *each of which is an instance of an established rule of inference or replacement.*

1. Thus, the validity of a formal proof depends on the rules that we will look at in the next lecture.
2. The validity of the rules depends on the definitions that we have lined out on the truth table.
3. The legitimacy of the truth table depends on the three laws of thought mentioned at the beginning of this lecture.

C. The tools established in this way can also be used to expedite the analysis of sets (as we shall see in Lecture Twenty-Two) and, further afield, to expedite the analysis of switching circuits and the construction of computer languages (where T and F are replaced by representations of "on" and "off" in binary arithmetic).

Essential Reading:

James Hall, *Logic Problems for Drill and Review*, Chapter 1, "The Apparatus," pp. 1–2.

Recommended Reading:

Irving Copi, *Introduction to Logic*, Chapter 8, "Symbolic Logic," pp. 299–320.

Questions to Consider:

1. If a truth table for a compound statement must have a row for every possible combination of truth values for all the compound's simple constituents (p, q, r, etc.), how many rows will be needed in the truth table for the following statement?

$$[(p \supset q) \bullet (q \supset r)] \supset (p \supset r)$$

Can you figure out a formula to determine how many rows are needed in a truth table for a compound statement with n simple constituents?

2. The equivalence symbol $\equiv$ ("triple bar") is often defined as follows:

$$p \equiv q \ \textit{means} \ (p \supset q) \bullet (q \supset p).$$

Can you construct a truth table for that definition statement?

93

Lecture Twenty
Modern Logic—Truth Tables

As we have seen, modern rational empiricism relies heavily upon hypothesis construction; upon theories; upon a mathematical apparatus; and upon devices, tools, and instruments—in all of its work, as we try to come to terms with, and understand and explain, the world around us and reality. What is out there, the world that we are trying to live in successfully? In order to do that, wherever the theories, and the hypotheses, and the mathematical apparatus come from, however we come by it, we need also an apparatus for inferring from the hypothesis to probable consequences. We need an apparatus that will allow us to move from A to B to C to D, reliably, and I shall not say effortlessly, but in an intelligible and straightforward way. Fortunately, we have that apparatus, and we have it in the form of modern logic. And what I am going to be doing in this lecture and in the next two lectures is introducing you to a quick sketch of what is involved in modern logic, modern symbolic logic. It is an extension of the old classical syllogistic logic of Aristotle that we talked about in Lectures Four through Lecture Seven. It connects very intimately with that, but it goes far beyond them.

Now, we are only going to be able to examine the rudiments of this vast system because it is vast and it is complicated. But I want to achieve in these three lectures for you to get the lay of the land, to have some understanding of what is going on. If you then want to pursue it, and I hope you will, you can find thorough treatments of modern symbolic logic in books that are recommended in the suggested readings that come with the lecture series. And if you have historical interests, you can find a brilliant exposition of the history and development of modern logic in William and Martha Neil's large and intriguing book, *The Development of Logic*.

Okay, let us begin by pointing out the distinct way that modern logic is related to, and at one with, classical Aristotelian syllogistic. It still holds to the three, as we call them, the laws of thought, which are the law of *identity*, the law of *non-contradiction*, and the law of *excluded middle* that we described when we were describing syllogistic logic many lectures ago. Let me recap for you quickly what those three laws of thought amount to because they are still crucial and central. The law of identity says that for any adequately explicit indicative descriptive sentence, whatever it may be, if it is true in a given context then it is going to be true throughout that context. If it is false in a given context, it is going to be false throughout that context. The truth value of a statement does not skitter around. It is what it is, and not something else. So, if it is raining here now, adequately explicit to a time and a place, if that is a true sentence in one line of your argument, then when that claim crops up again in another line of your argument, the truth value will be the same. If it is false, the truth value will be the same. As an aside, just anticipating something that is going to come up very shortly, we could, of course, always talk about some specific sentence, like "It is raining (here, now)," or "Today is Wednesday." It is much more convenient to adopt a very simple convention and use a variable to represent any old simple sentence. And so I am going to be using the lower-case letter q and the lower-case letter p simply as variables or place markers. And so when I say, "Consider the simple indicative sentence p, you realize that that p is a place marker, and you could plug any simple indicative sentence in its place at will.

The law of non-contradiction says that for any adequately explicit indicative descriptive sentence p, if it is true in a given context then its denial in that context must be false. And if it is false in a given context, then its denial must be true. So, an assertion and the denial of that same assertion cannot have the same truth value. The law of identity, the law of non-contradiction, and, finally, the law of excluded middle for any adequately specific descriptive indicative sentence p, the only alternative truth values that are available are "True" and "False." There is no "tertium quid." There is no third option, not in this system.

Now, these three laws of thought as they are practiced currently are not viewed as self-evidently true pronouncements about the ultimate nature of the world as it has to be. They are simply understood as the rules of the game. They are the basic postulates on which the entire apparatus is hung. Because of that, the law of identity, the law of non-contradiction, and the law of excluded middle constitute a very basic assumption—notice, assumption—about the nature of the world or reality out there, namely that it is coherent. If that assumption is not correct, if the world is not coherent, then all bets are off, and the system would be of no use to us whatever.

Now, these three laws of thought are going to be useful to us in constructing something that I will put up on the computer screen shortly in graphic format, something called a "truth table." And you will see a truth table shortly. On a truth table, using the three laws of thought that we have been talking about, what I am going to do is to define some logical operators or some logical symbols that we can use in representing different ways to connect simple sentences together. If you have a couple of simple sentences p and q, you might connect them together in a variety of ways. You might connect them together in terms of what we call *conjunction, and*, and I will introduce a dot as a symbol representing that on a truth table. They might be connected by what we call *disjunction, or*, and I will introduce this, a symbol called a *wedge*, which we will use to represent *or* on a truth table. Similarly, I am going to introduce you to several other symbols to represent *implication*, you will see it in a minute and one is called a horseshoe, and I am going to introduce a symbol that says "if and only if," implied both ways, which we call a triple bar.

Let me go ahead and get the first, simplest truth table up on the screen, and it is a truth table for *negation*. I want to take the time to talk about the truth table itself for a moment because a lot depends on this. I want you to notice that the truth table has several parts. On the left-hand side of this truth table for negation, we find a column under the letter p. P is a variable representing any old statement you like. We find a column under that of the possible truth values of such a statement. Given our three laws of thought, there are only two of them. There are only two possible truth values for a simple statement: T represents True, and F represents False. And they are put successively in two rows on the column under p. Now, that guide column, as we call it, is going to determine the value of p on the same row over on the right-hand side, however many times p crops up. Now, in the instance that we have on the screen right now, it is a very simple example because what is over on the right-hand side, the statement that we are going to try to evaluate is simply the denial of p, and we are introducing the curl, the little tilde in front of the p, to represent denial. It simply means "not." So we do not have a lot of iteration of p's and other letters on this truth table. We just have a guide column for p itself. Over on the right-hand side, we have *curl p*, not p, and we define the curl in that column of values under *curl p* on the right-hand side. Where p is True, *curl p* is False. Where p is

False, *curl p* is True, and that is nothing more than a graphic representation of the law of non-contradiction—that an assertion and its denial cannot have the same value, that whatever value a statement has, its denial has the opposite one. So there is a nice, simple truth table—guide column on the left, statement to be evaluated on the right. In this instance, there is only one variable in play, only one statement, and we have defined the curl or the tilde to represent denial or negation.

The next truth table is a little bit more complicated because on the next truth table the first thing you will notice is that in the left-hand or guide columns we have got values for two variables. We have values under *p*, and we have got values under *q*, and it may strike you as odd that the values have been laid out in the way that they are laid out, so let me talk about that for a moment. If you are only talking about one statement, then there are only two possibilities. It is either going to be True, or it is going to be False—one or the other. If you have two statements, then there are four possibilities. They might both be True. The first one might be True, and the second one False. The first one might be False, and the second one True. Or they might both be False. What the guide columns on the left-hand side of this truth table represent are the four possible combinations of truth values for two variables. With the variable *p* and the variable *q* both True; first True, second False; first False second True; both False. That exhausts the possibilities. Time out while you digest that.

Every additional variable that you add to your truth table is going to double the number of possible combinations of truth values for any statement that you are working with. So if you had not just *p* and *q*, but *p* and *q* and *r*, then there would be eight possible combinations—all the way from all three of them are True down to all three of them are False, and everything in between. If you had *p* and *q* and *r* and *s*, you would have 16 combinations. Now, you can do the doubling and doubling. It is very scary because as you add more variables, the truth table guide columns rapidly become extremely cumbersome and difficult to work with. Consequently, as I assure my students in my logic classes, we do not want to work with truth tables any longer than we have to. We are going to work with truth tables while they are relatively small and relatively simple.

If you want to get a convenient way, if you are setting up a truth table for yourself, figure out how many rows you are going to need in terms of how many variables you have. It is going to be two to the nth power, n being the number of variables that you have. That is how many rows you need, and in the one that is closest to the right, simply alternate T's and F's until you have that many. Then drop back one column, and alternate T's and F's in duets; drop back another column, and alternate T's and F's in quartets, and so on. You will find an array that covers the possibilities nicely. Here, there are only two variables, so we have True, True; True, False; False, True; False, False. We are defining a connector here called the "dot," for the relationship of the conjunction "and." Well, not just "and"—also "but," "also," "furthermore," "in addition"—there are a lot of words in English that express what we are capturing with the dot. The dot captures the common meaning of all of those different words for conjunction that we use.

Furthermore, and let me notice this with "and," because it is going to become very important with "if...then" in just a moment; we capture the common meaning of all these different conjunctive words, but we only capture the common partial meaning. There are contexts in which the word "and" in English says more than both parts are True. There are contexts, in English, where the word "and" says not only both parts are True, but says something about the sequence in which those events occur. As my mother would have noted, there is all the difference in the world between John and Sue getting married and having a baby, and John and Sue having a baby and getting married. And in English, the word "and" often says something about sequencing. It is important to realize in the logical apparatus, that the dot does not say anything about sequencing at all. All the dot captures is the claim that both parts are True. Having said that, you would already know what is in the column under the statement before you even look. Here $P \cdot Q$ is going to be True on the first row. It is going to be True where both parts are True. It is not True on the second row, because Q is False. It is not True on the third row because P is False. It is not True on the last row because both of them are False. Then $P \cdot Q$ is True "if and only if" both components are True. That is the common partial meaning of conjunction.

This truth table has the same structure as the one we were just looking at, but I am introducing another connector here. The word that is used is "disjunction," and maybe you can remember that in contrast to conjunction; if conjunction puts things together, disjunction sort of stretches things apart and separates them. We represent it with what is called a "wedge." Loosely speaking, the wedge represents the English word "or," but I am going to have to say something to that momentarily. Notice that the guide columns are identical to the ones we used for the dot. With two variables, p and q, they can both be True; first one True and second one False; etcetera. There is no change. Over under the statement P, wedge Q, we find a very different set of values because we find P wedge Q is True on the first three rows of the truth table. It is True where they are both True. It is True where the first one is True. It is True where the second one is True. The only place where it is False is where both of them are False. That captures pretty well what we mean in English by the word "or," or at least it captures what we mean by the word "or" in what is called its *inclusive sense*.

Now there are occasions in English where when we say p or q we mean one or the other, but not both. That is called *exclusive disjunction* and is relatively rare. There are places where we clearly mean at least one, possibly both. That is called *inclusive disjunction*. The wedge represents inclusive disjunction. You can figure it out, and I will leave it to you as an exercise; I will just talk it through, but you can do it on paper; if you wanted to represent p or q, but not both p and q it would be easy. You would write "p wedge q" and then you would write "and," and then you would write "not." Then you would write "p and q," one or the other, but not both. And if you checked out the truth values on that, you would find that it would be True only where exactly one component is True; it would be False on the first row as well as on the last. The wedge captures the common partial meaning of this junction in English.

An aside: Precise meanings can get very crucial in contracts. That is why lawyers drive us all crazy by writing things like "and," or "or" into a contract that they are drawing up, to make it very clear that they mean inclusive disjunction. Or they will write one or the other, but not both exclusively, or something like that when they want it very clear that they mean exclusive disjunction. In everyday discourse, we tend to be a little looser than that.

The horseshoe, which I am introducing on this truth table, broadly speaking, represents the English phrase "if…then." So, if we want to say "if p then q" we would write as we have at the top of the truth table, the right-hand side, p horseshoe q. Notice that the guide columns here are exactly the same as they were in the last two truth tables. We are still working with two variables. As long as we are working with two variables, those guide columns will never change. Combinations are both True; one True, the other False; one False the other True; and both False. Those are all of the possibilities there are. Over under the statement under the horseshoe I have written in the values of the "if…then" statement as the horseshoe is defined.

But I need to talk to you about that for a moment. And this is why I wanted to talk about common partial meaning earlier on. There are dozens of different expressions in English that amount to something like "if…then." Sometimes we say that "p causes q," and that is a way of saying that "if p happens, then q happens." Sometimes we say that "p and q are statistically correlated in such a way that p does not occur without q; so if p happens, q happens." And there are many other flavors of "if…thens" in English, and they are quite different. It is very different to say that two things are merely statistically correlated on the one hand, and to say that there is a tight causal relationship with them on the other. What we want in the logical system is an operator that will represent what all of those different "if…thens" have in common, what they all have in common. And so we ask ourselves, "What does p cause as q have in common with p logically entails q, and have in common with p is inexorably statistically associated with q, and all of the other possible if p then qs that there might be?" And there is one thing that they do have in common. Every one of them is False if p occurs in the absence of q. To say, if p, then q—whether we mean causal, statistical, coincidental, logical—you do not get p without q. The assertion that p is True and q is False is out. Notice on the truth table under the statement "p horseshoe q" that is where the only F shows up. The claim "p horseshoe q" is False, if and only if p is True and q is False.

That leads to, what are called by some, "the paradoxes of material implication." Namely that "p horseshoe q" turns out to be True on the third and forth lines, where p itself is False. But, if you stop and think about it, if p itself is not True, then certainly p itself does not occur in the absence of q. If it does not occur at all, it does not occur in the absence of q. And if that is what the horseshoe is capturing, that p does not occur in the absence of q, then that is True, where p does not occur. So, the common partial meaning of a wide variety of "if…then" is captured rather nicely by the horseshoe, not quite as intuitively as the dot and the wedge for "and," and for "or."

The last truth table that I am going to show you today—there will be some more in the next lecture—is for a connector, again between two variables *p* and *q*. The connector is called a triple bar. What that connector really means—and we will see this on a larger truth table—is p implies q, and q implies p. They imply each other. The triple bar is shorthand, then, for p horseshoe q, and q horseshoe p. But, I am not going to define it in terms of the double-barreled, two-direction horseshoes. I am going to define it very straightforwardly, and then we will have fun in the next session, seeing how defined this way meshes like a hand in a glove with the way we will treat it next time. Look at your guide columns again. There are two variables, no change from anything we have seen so far. P and q are both True, or p is True and q is False, or p is False and q is True, or they are both False. Those are all of the options there are. P triple bar q? Well, it says that p triple bar q is True where they are both True, and it is True where they are both False, but p triple bar q is False when they are different. So, another way to read the triple bar as well as "if and only if" is equivalence. P triple bar q is a way of saying they have got the same truth value, and that truth value might be True, as it is on the first row, or it might be False, as it is on the last row. If they are the same, then the triple bar statement is True, but where p and q differ in truth value, p triple bar q shows up False.

Now, with just these operators—the curl, the dot, the wedge, the horseshoe, and the triple bar—we can symbolize sentences, compound sentences of really incredible complexity. As we will see in the next section, we can proceed using truth tables again. We can proceed to establish some rules in terms of which we can verify that certain conclusions follow from certain premises.

In the next lecture, we are going to see how we can, using truth tables, establish equivalencies between different statements, so that we can make substitutions, and we are going to establish some rules of inference so that we can draw conclusions from premises validly. And this puts us in a position to offer a nice, tight definition in modern logic of a valid argument, as we shall see. *An argument is valid if and only if its conclusion can be derived from its premises in a finite number of steps, where every step that we take has been nailed in place and demonstrated on the truth table already.* So the validity of a formal proof depends upon the rules that we are going to be looking at in our next session. The validity of the rules depends on the definitions that we have lined out on the truth table. What does the legitimacy of the truth table depend on? It depends on the three laws of thought. The legitimacy of the truth table depends on the claim that where p is True, it is True; where it is False, it is False; where it is not True, it is False; where it is not False, it is True—and those are the only options there are.

So we have a skyhook, if you please. The laws of thought on which by definition we suspend the logical operators and the truth table definitions, we then use those to establish rules of inference and rules of substation. We then use those to establish formal proofs. And what if the laws of thought are wrong? Well, as I said at the beginning of today's lecture, they presume that the world is coherent, that the world makes sense. If the world is not coherent, if the presumption behind the laws of thought is improper, if the world—as Ionesco would have it—is absurd, then all bets are off. We can forget logic and all go see Rhinoceros.

Lecture Twenty-One
Modern Logic—Sentential Arguments

Scope:

Using the basic logical connectives as defined on truth tables, representations of a statement can often be expressed in alternative equivalent ways. Using truth tables, a number of such equivalences can be justified as *replacement rules* that allow one equivalent statement to replace another. Traditionally, there are 10 or so replacement rules, such as *DeMorgan's theorems, transposition,* and *exportation. Rules of inference* are demonstrable on truth tables, too. They include *modus ponens, hypothetical syllogism,* and 8 or so others. Many of the rules are readily derived from the others as theorems. With both kinds of rules in place, complex logical derivations are possible and secure. It is important to note, however, that these derivations are only "truth preserving." Nothing in the system provides any assurance that the premises of any argument are true.

Outline

I. The logical force of statements can often be captured in alternative ways.

    A. When that is the case, the alternatives are always equivalent to each other in truth value.

    B. Based on truth table demonstrations, it is easy to show that certain statements are equivalent in this way. Here are two examples:

One of DeMorgan's Two Theorems							
p	*q*	~(*p*	∨	*q*) ≡	(~*p*	•	~*q*)
T	T	F	T	**T**	F	F	F
T	F	F	T	**T**	F	F	T
F	T	F	T	**T**	T	F	F
F	F	T	F	**T**	T	T	T

"Neither *p* nor *q*, if and only if, not *p* and not *q*."

Material Implication						
p	q	\multicolumn{5}{l}{$(p \supset q) \equiv (\sim p \lor q)$}

p	q	$(p$	$\supset$	$q)$	$\equiv$	$(\sim p$	$\lor$	$q)$
T	T	T	**T**	F	T	T
T	F	F	**T**	F	F	F
F	T	T	**T**	T	T	T
F	F	T	**T**	T	T	F

"If p then q, if and only if, not p unless q."

C. On the left-hand side are the guide columns, and there, we find all the possible combinations of true and false values for the two variables p and q. On the right side are the statements, and we can fill in the values on the right-hand side for all the possible values of p and q as indicated by the guide columns.

II. Ten or so such equivalences are traditionally identified as *replacement rules* that allow their equivalent statements to be substituted for each other at will. We shall look at five samples.

A. *DeMorgan's two theorems:* Denying a conjunction says that at least one of its parts is false and vice versa, and denying a disjunction says that both of its parts are false and vice versa.

$\sim(p \bullet q) \equiv (\sim p \lor \sim q)$ and $\sim(p \lor q) \equiv (\sim p \bullet \sim q)$

B. *Exportation:* A sequence of conditionals can be clustered, and a cluster can be sequenced.

$[p \supset (q \supset r)] \equiv [(p \bullet q) \supset r]$

C. *Transposition:* A conditional can be reversed if you change the signs of both terms:

$(p \supset q) \equiv (\sim q \supset \sim p)$

D. *Material implication:* Saying that P is a sufficient condition of Q is the same as saying that it is not the case that Q occurs in the absence of P or that P does not occur unless Q does.

$(p \supset q) \equiv \sim(p \bullet \sim q)$ or $(p \supset q) \equiv (\sim p \lor q)$

E. *Tautology:* You need not repeat yourself, but you may if you like.

$p \equiv (p \bullet p)$ and $p \equiv (p \lor p)$

III. It is demonstrable on truth tables that certain inference patterns are valid; that is, the conclusion is never false when the premises are true. For example (using /∴ to mean "therefore"):

Modus Ponens ("powerful method")					
p	*q*	*p* ⊃ *q*	*p*	/∴ *q*	
T	T	**T**	**T**	T	√
T	F	F	T	F	
F	T	T	F	T	
F	F	T	F	T	

Example of *modus ponens*: If you love me, you will remember our anniversary. You do love me. Therefore, you will remember our anniversary.

Absorption					
p	*q*	*p* ⊃ *q*	/∴ *p* ⊃ (*p* • *q*)		
T	T	**T**	**T**	T	√
T	F	F	F	F	
F	T	**T**	**T**	F	√
F	F	**T**	**T**	F	√

Example of absorption: If today is Wednesday, then I have an appointment at 4:00. So it follows that if today is Wednesday, then today is Wednesday, and I have an appointment at 4:00.

IV. Ten or so such patterns are traditionally identified as *inference rules*. Here are seven (again using /∴ to mean "therefore"):

A. *Modus ponens*

$p \supset q$

p /∴ q

B. *Absorption*

$p \supset q$ /∴ $p \supset (p \bullet q)$

C. *Simplification*

$$p \bullet q \qquad /\therefore \quad p$$

D. *Conjunction*

$$p$$

$$q \qquad /\therefore \; p \bullet q$$

E. *Hypothetical syllogism (chain argument)*

$$p \supset q$$

$$q \supset r \qquad /\therefore \quad p \supset r$$

F. *Reductio*

$$p \supset (q \bullet \sim q) \quad /\therefore \quad \sim p$$

G. *Conditional proof*

One may assume a hypothesis and infer from it and the premises together. Then, upon discharging the hypothesis, one may infer the conditional: *If this hypothesis is made, this result follows.*

V. Only a few of the usual rules are essential, the others being readily derived from them as theorems. For instance, hypothetical syllogism can be (laboriously) derived from the others.

   A. Absorption is essential. It cannot be derived from the other rules, and certain valid arguments cannot be proved without it.

   B. While the traditional rule set is not as parsimonious as it might be, it has the advantage of closely tracking the syntax of many natural languages, including English.

   C. There is a judgment call involved in deciding how many rules to include. Having lots of rules makes for short proofs but gives us many principles to keep track of. Just a few rules are easy to handle, but the proofs get long. The traditional system is a compromise.

VI. With replacement and inference rules in place, complex derivations are possible, such as:

   A.

1. $p \supset q$		
2. $p \supset (q \supset r)$	$/\therefore$	$\mathbf{P} \supset \mathbf{R}$
3. $p \supset (p \bullet q)$	1	Absorption
4. $(p \bullet q) \supset r$	3	Exportation

5. $p \supset r$ 2, 4   Hyp. Syllogism

B. 1. $p \supset (q \bullet r)$ /∴ $P \supset Q$
   2. p Hypothesis
   3. $q \bullet r$ 1, 2   *Modus Ponens*
   4. q 3   Simplification
   5. $p \supset q$ 2-4   Conditional Proof

VII.   The inferences sanctioned by these rules are only truth *preserving*—that is, they will safely keep whatever truth we start with, but that is all. Whether the premises with which an argument begins are true is an entirely *extra-logical* matter.

   A. One can construct proofs for one's premises, but that will require further premises.

   B. One could hope for "self-evident" premises, but that is a dicey hope.

   C. The normal way to determine whether a premise is true is to consult experience. That is why this whole approach is called *rational empiricism*, not just *rationalism*.

Essential Reading:

James Hall, *Logic Problems for Drill and Review*, Chapter 1, "The Apparatus," pp. 3–11.

Recommended Reading:

Irving Copi, *Introduction to Logic*, Chapter 9, "The Method of Deduction," pp. 349–371.

Questions to Consider:

1. What is the practical advantage of proving an argument by using the rules, as compared to constructing a truth table for the argument as a whole?

2. Does not finding a way to demonstrate an argument by using the rules constitute any sort of proof that the argument is invalid (or even likely to be invalid)? If not, how could you show that a complex argument is invalid (short of constructing *large* truth tables)? After you have thought about this, look at pages 372–375 in Copi's *Introduction to Logic*.

3. See whether you understand the steps in the following argument (the first three statements are premises):

1. $p \supset q$
2. $m \supset \sim q$
3. $\sim(p \cdot z)$
4. $\sim z \supset m$ $/\therefore$ $\sim p$
5. $\sim p \vee \sim z$ 3   DeMorgan's Theorem
6. $p \supset \sim z$ 5   Material Implication
7. $p \supset m$ 6, 4   Hyp. Syllogism
8. $p \supset \sim q$ 7, 2   Hyp. Syllogism
9. $q \supset \sim p$ 8   Transposition
10. $p \supset \sim p$ 1, 10   Hyp. Syllogism
11. $\sim p \vee \sim p$ 10   Material Implication
12. $\sim p$ 11   Tautology

Lecture Twenty-One
Modern Logic—Sentential Arguments

In the last lecture, I used truth tables to introduce and to define some logical operators: the curl, the wedge, the dot, the horseshoe, and the triple bar for "not," "or," "and," "if then," and "if and only if," respectively. We can use those logical operators to symbolize or represent sentences in ordinary English arguments, and when we do that, we discover very, very quickly that the same sentence can often be expressed in more than one equivalent way. And the equivalence of certain sentences can also be demonstrated very nicely on truth tables, as we shall now see.

On your screen or in the study guide, you will see a truth table labeled "One of DeMorgan's Theorems." Now, let me remind you a little bit about truth tables. On the left-hand side are the guide columns, and there we find all the possible combinations of values for two variables "p" and "q"—both True; one True, the other False; and so on. Over to the right, we have a rather lengthy and complicated statement written. Reading it out in English, what that statement says, "neither p nor q, if and only if, not p and not q." Following the definitions of the curl, the wedge, the triple bar, and the dot, we can fill in the values on the right-hand side of this truth table for all the possible values of p and q as indicated by the guide columns. Thus, under the wedge on the left-hand side of the triple bar, we have the values for p or q—True on all the lines except the last one, but that is denied. There is a negation sign outside the parenthesis, so that reverse is the value, all False except the last one, and so on.

The point is, that when you work this out methodically, step by step, you discover when you go to fill in the values under the triple bar that they come up True every time—neither p nor q, on the one hand, and both not p and not q, on the other hand, ride together. They inevitably have the same truth value. They are interchangeable.

Here is another example—guide columns on the left as usual. Over on the right-hand side, I have "if p then q, if and only if, not p unless q." Methodically, we would fill in the values under the horseshoe. We would fill in the values under the "not p" and the wedge. When we are done and go to fill in the values under the triple bar, we discover it comes up True every time. To say "if p, then q," and to say "not p unless q," is to say the same thing as far as their truth values are concerned. They are interchangeable. This gives us a very, very powerful tool as we begin to analyze and run arguments, because it means where we know that certain statements are interchangeable, are equivalent, we can unplug one and plug in the other in its place, if that is convenient or useful for us to do, without having any impact on the truth value of the argument at all. Thus, this kind of demonstration on truth tables generates what we call "Substitution Rules."

Now, with the Substitution Rules or "Replacement Rules," there are about 10 of them, usually in most logical systems. That is an adjustable number. It depends on what you are setting the system up for and how many rules you like, but there are usually about 10— two of those we have just looked at: one of *DeMorgan's theorems* and the definition of *material implication*.

Here are both of DeMorgan's theorems, and I am not going to do the truth tables now, I just want to illustrate to you what the Substitution Rules look like. The first one, which we have already seen, says, "neither p nor q, if and only if, not p and not q." The other one says, "It's not the case that both p and q together, if and only if, at least one of them is False—that is either not p or not q." DeMorgan's theorems allow us, among other things, to move the negation sign, which you will notice is outside the parenthesis in the left-hand statement, move it inside the parenthesis, and when we do, change the connection between the terms so that the deniable of a disjunction becomes the conjunction of two denials. The denial of a conjunction becomes the disjunction of two denials. And those substitutions are often very, very useful.

There are other Substitution Rules as well. Let me show you just a few of them. Here is one called *exportation*. What exportation amounts to is that if you have a string of conditionals that are sufficient to get you to a certain conclusion, as on the left-hand side of the triple bar, "if p, then if q, then r," you can export or cluster those conditions together into a clump and say "if p and q together, then r." You can stretch them out or compress them at will. It makes no difference in the truth value of the statement at all.

Transposition is yet another. Transposition is a very, very useful rule because it allows us to turn an "if...then" statement around. But when we do, we have to change the truth value of both ends of the statement. See what happens. "P horseshoe q" can be turned around and becomes "not q, horseshoe, not p." Let me digress on that one for just a moment. We could show this on a truth table easily, but you can also see it very, very clearly just in words. It is perfectly True that if something is a cocker spaniel, then it is a dog. It is not perfectly True that if something is a dog, then it is a cocker spaniel. You can't just turn the "if…then" around. But since it is True that if it is a cocker spaniel then it is a dog, you can transpose it and say, "If it is not a dog, then it is not a cocker spaniel." That ought to remind you of something from back around Lecture Seven or Lecture Eight called *contraposition*. It is exactly the same thing, but captured now in terms of "if…thens," and "if and only ifs."

Material implication—that is, the horseshoe itself—can be defined on truth tables several different equivalent ways. I have two of them for you to look at in your study guide or on the screen. The one on top says, "p horseshoe q is the same as, is equivalent to, is interchangeable with, not p unless q." The one on the bottom says, "p horseshoe q is interchangeable with"; it is not the case that "p and not q." So, you could say, "not p unless q," or you could say "It is not the case that p happens without q"—either way, you are saying the same thing; either way you are saying "If p, then q." There are three different ways to express this notion that one thing is a sufficient condition of another, and which way you want to express it may very well depend upon the particular context of the argument in which you are working. So the Substitution Rules work on that.

One last one that I love is called *tautology*, and it says that, "p is equivalent to p and p"; also that, "p is equivalent to p or p." I like to think of this rule as saying you don't have to repeat yourself, but you may if you like because there are certain contexts in an argument where it is useful to generate multiple iterations of the same letter. And there are operations in arguments where although you don't want it to happen, multiple iterations of the same level occur, and you need to sweep them out and get them out of the way. And the rule of tautology says it doesn't matter how many times you say it— one, two, 11, or 500. It is all the same.

Now, not only can we generate with our truth-table techniques some Substitution Rules or some Replacement Rules that allow us to unplug one statement and replace it with another statement that is a truth-functional equivalent—with our truth tables, we also can establish some very, very basic Rules of Inference. Let me start with the most basic Rule of Inference and work through that one with you, and then we will look briefly at several others just to get a feeling for the lay of the land, of what sorts of things are available.

This Rule of Inference is called *modus ponens*—which, if my Latin is at all correct, means something like "powerful method," and it is a powerful method indeed. Let me give you an example of *modus ponens*. If today is Wednesday, then I have an appointment at 4:00 o'clock. Today is Wednesday, so I have an appointment at 4:00. If you love me, you will remember our anniversary. You do love me; therefore, you will remember our anniversary. I'd better. There are thousands, and thousands, and thousands of arguments, which all alike share the structure of *modus ponens*. What you will see in your study guide or on the screen is a skeletal representation of the form of *modus ponens* using variables, using p and q again. But you could generate real arguments out of this by substituting real statements for the p and the q. Guide columns are on the left, same as ever.

Over on the right this time, I have created a column for the two premises of the argument. There is a column for "if p, then q"; there is a column for p; and there is a slash and three dots, that reads "therefore," and over on the very far right, there is a column for the conclusion. And what I want to do, systematically, is to figure out what is the truth value of the components of each of those lines, which I've done; "p horseshoe q" is False on the second row, but True on the rest; p and q have the truth values that the guide columns established for them. And then what I want to do to see if this argument is valid is to identify any rows on the truth table where the premises are all True. And in this case, there is only one. On the first row of the truth table, both premises are True. On the other rows, one premise or another is False. And notice that I've marked it in red for you, that on the one line where both of the premises are True, the conclusion is True as well. It is impossible for "p horseshoe q" to be True and p to be True unless q is True as well. So, the skeleton form *modus ponens* is valid. It is impossible for its premises to be True without its conclusion being True also, and since that skeleton form is valid, any instance of it is valid—*modus ponens*, a basic and important fundamental Rule of Inference.

I will show you one more on the truth table. It is called *absorption*, and it is an odd one because it is one you would never think of using

©2005 The Teaching Company Limited Partnership

in everyday life or the real world, but it's one that for technical reasons is quite important. This says that, "if p implies q, that is your premise, you may infer that p implies itself and q together." Well, duh. Let's see, if today is Wednesday, then I have an appointment at 4:00, so it follows if today is Wednesday, then today is Wednesday, and I have an appointment at 4:00. Well, yes, and you can work through the truth table and the lines where "p horseshoe q" is True—that is the first, the third and the fourth—the conclusion is True as well, marked in red. It is impossible for "if p, then q" to be True without "if p, then p and q being True" at the same time.

Let me digress for a second. I can't dwell on this. It's an interesting question, and I alluded to it a moment ago, "How many rules shall we have?" And if we had time, I could show you that many of the rules that are used can be derived from other rules—that is, we frequently have more rules in play then we really, necessarily need. I bring this up simply to point out that this curious "Rule of Absorption" cannot be derived from the others. You cannot derive it as a theorem using the other rules as axioms in the system. It simply cannot be done. It's absolutely free-standing, and there are valid arguments—demonstrable, valid arguments; demonstrable on truth tables—that cannot be established without the use of this rule. So, as odd as it looks and as strange as it sounds, this is one of the rules that has to be in the system no matter what, absorption. There are many, many Rules of Inference; usually in most systems about a dozen are in play. We have looked at *modus ponens* and absorption so far. Let me direct your attention to one or two others.

Simplification, a very, very straight forward rule, but an important one: If you know that two things are True—they are connected with a dot in a premise—you may break them apart and take one of them out by itself on a separate line. You may simplify. So, "if p and q" is True, it follows that p is True. And, in reverse, if you know that p is True, and you walk around the block, and you come back, and you look, and you discover, well, q is True, then you can put them together on the same line and join them with a dot. If p is known to be True, q is known to be True, and then you may infer p and q.

The next one I purposely have not done on a truth table because it's got three variables in it, and the truth table would have eight rows. I recommend that you try that. It's a lot of fun to set it up. You know how to do it; we talked about that last time. The argument form, the forest, is a very familiar one to you. You have used this form of argument probably since kindergarten days. If p implies q, and q implies r, what is the connection between p and r? Well, it goes through. The classical name for this is *hypothetical syllogism*; the common everyday name for this is *chain argument*. Chain argument, just like the links of a chain; if one thing leads to another, and that leads to a third, it passes through. And you may say, "if the first, then the last." So, if p implies q, and q implies r, you may infer that p implies r.

The last thing that we will look at for just a moment is a very, very important rule. It is called *reductio*, and it is a rule that goes way, way back in human thinking to the time of Euclid. What reductio says, look at it carefully, reductio says that, "if p implies a contradiction—if p implies both q and not q—you may infer that p is not the case." So, if p implies absurdities, then p just ain't so. And that is exactly what Euclid did in his geometrical proofs when he would say, "Let's hypothesize that the shortest distance between two points is not a straight line," and show that that hypothesis led to absurdities, 2 + 2 = 7, and he would then say, "Which is absurd? Therefore, the hypothesis is False"; therefore, the shortest distance between two points is a straight line on his analysis.

Reductio is an extremely powerful tool of inference. By the way, it is not an essential one. It can be derived from the other rules as a theorem quite readily. But it is so useful, and it is so tight, that you will usually find it on your list of rules and find it being put to heavy, heavy use.

Finally, on the rules, there is a procedure called *conditional proof* that I will demonstrate for you in just a moment when I run a proof. But I want to show you a way to use these rules together in a proof that does not involve conditional proof first. Then we will look at one that does.

Here is a proof—and let's imagine an argument to go with this. If today is Wednesday, then I have an appointment at 4:00—if today is Wednesday, then if I have an appointment at 4:00, and I had better leave by 3:30. Therefore, if today is Wednesday, then I had better leave by 3:30. P implies q; p implies that q implies r; therefore, p implies r. We could prove the validity of this on a truth table itself if we chose to. It would be a truth table with eight rows. It would be fairly complicated. Remember, every additional variable that goes into the truth table, the truth table doubles in size. Doubles. So that the time you have an argument with say 10 variables in it, your truth table is well north of a thousand rows long. So, truth tables are not efficient for large arguments.

But instead of proving this on a truth table, what I am going to do is appeal to three rules that we have already talked about that are themselves readily demonstrable on truth tables. The first thing I am going to do is to take that first line, "p implies q," and apply the Rule of Absorption to it, and say that since p implies q, I may infer by the Rule of Absorption that p implies p and q together. And that is secure.

On line four, I am going to look back up at line two, and I am going to say, "If p implies that q implies r by exportation, I may say that p and q, together, imply r." So, I am exporting, clustering up together, the conditions stated in line two. But now look what I have got on lines three and four. Line three says that p implies a certain conjunction. Line four says that very same conjunction implies r. So, by chain argument, or by hypothetical syllogism, it goes through from three and four, I can establish p implies r. Voila. It is demonstrated in three steps, each step of which is iron clad, demonstrable on a truth table. That is the essential core of formal proof construction in modern logic—to show that from a set of premises, you can get to a conclusion in a finite number of steps, where each step that you take is an instance of a Rule of Inference or a Substitution Rule that has been demonstrated on a truth table.

Now I mentioned that there was another technique that we can use and that we will use. It is called *conditional proof.* Let me take a moment to explain to you what is going on here. Sometimes in an argument, we have some premises, and we are trying to get to a conclusion, and sometimes it is useful to hypothesize some additional piece of information to ask ourselves, "Well, what if such and so were the case, where could we get on that hypothesis?" We have been talking for any number of sessions now about the role of hypothesis construction in scientific inquiry—offering hypotheses to see where they will lead us is mother's milk to scientific inquiry. So, in an argument, we are allowed to hypothesize if we like, and then see what we can derive from the premises that are given and our hypothesis working together.

Here is an example on the screen or in your study guide. My premise is that p implies q and r, and what I want to establish is that p implies q all by itself. Now, intuitively, that is pretty straightforward. If today is Tuesday, then I have an appointment at 3:00 and a party this evening. Therefore, if today is today, I have an appointment at 3:00. But there is no single Rule of Inference that will get us from that premise to that conclusion. It is a little bit more complicated than that. I could go through agonies of unpacking the premise, take it apart with Substitution Rules, multiply it through, do distributions like you used to do in arithmetic. I could shake that conclusion out. But it is so much easier to simply hypothesize p, and say, "Well, what if p were the case? I am going to hypothesize that and see what I get." So I mark that on line two with a red arrow, and I write my hypothesis off to the right, and if I do that, then immediately from the premise and the hypothesis together, I can get q and r by *modus ponens*. And if I have got q and r on line three, then I can simplify that to get q all by itself.

So, what have I discovered? I have discovered that if you hypothesize p, then you can get q, because that is what I just did. I hypothesized p and got q. So, I bend my hypothesis arrow back across. I discharge that hypothesis and let it go and write down what I have just demonstrated reading line five with care. If you hypothesize p, then you can get q—and the justification for that is, lines two through four taken together and the principle of conditional proof.

Now, as I said to you a few moments ago, only a few of these rules are absolutely essential. It's a very, very interesting exercise in logic to see how few rules you can get by with. And that is a very, very instructive enterprise, to take the set of rules that are stated in some standard logic textbook like Copi—which is the text book I always use when I am teaching a logic class to undergraduates—and there are Copi's 18 rules—and ask yourself, "How many of these could I get rid of? How many of these could I derive as theorems from the others?" And you can pare the list down to a very, very small set. You pay an interesting price if you do, and this is worth noting. The fewer rules you have in your system, the longer your proofs get, because with a very small set of tools, you have to do lots and lots of iterative and reiterative work. And a very simple proof using 18 or 19 rules might turn out to be literally hundreds of lines long if you only had one or two rules to work with.

Conversely, you can make every proof one line long. All you have to do is have infinitely many rules. Just identify every argument that was ever voiced, prove it on a truth table, and give it a name, and then any time you run into that argument again, you can say, "Oh yes, that is argument number 17,942,113, and as we know on the truth table of the same number, that is valid." Lots of rules, short proofs. Tiny number of rules, long proofs. It's a judgment call. About how many rules can we remember and work with comfortably? About how big are we comfortable with the problems and the proofs being? And so, a judgment call gets made.

The wonderful thing about this apparatus is that it allows us to mechanically construct proofs and demonstrations even in areas where we don't have strong first-hand knowledge of the information that we are arguing about. This is a very, very important point. And it is the point on which this lecture will end. Let me put it this way. Good logic is truth *preserving*, and that is all it is. If you do your logic right, then whatever truth you start out with you will preserve through to the end. But logic will not create truth, nor will it discover truth. It will only preserve whatever truth you have. So, you can go to work on an argument even if you don't understand the niceties of the claims that are occurring in it, and you can simply see whether or not the conclusion of that argument follows from those assumptions. And if your logic is right, you will know that you are not going to be losing any truth along the way.

Now, at a practical level, I suppose it would be very nice if we always only argued from True premises, or if we had some way of guaranteeing that the premises we are arguing from are True. But logic just can't do that for us, and the hope that we might find self-evident truths somewhere seems like a forlorn hope anymore. So, we have to satisfy ourselves with the notion that however much truth we start out with, "if we mind our p's and q's," as the logicians say, we can be sure that we will preserve that truth through to the end.

Lecture Twenty-Two
Modern Logic—Predicate Arguments

Scope:

One of the strengths of modern logic is that it clearly establishes the relationship between predicate logic (e.g., syllogisms) and sentential argument forms, such as *modus ponens*. Using simple conventions for representing predication, the Boolean interpretation of universals, two new operators (the universal and particular quantifiers to express general claims), and two new rules for instantiating (applying) general claims to individuals, predicate arguments far beyond the scope of Aristotelian syllogistic can be solved, utilizing all of the power of the apparatus introduced for handling sentential arguments.

Outline

I. *Sentential arguments*, as in the last lecture, depend upon the connections between simple sentences joined with such connectors as "and," "or," and "if then." In *predicate arguments*, everything depends upon the relationship between the subject and predicate terms within a sentence.

II. Modern logic connects predicate arguments and sentential arguments, such as *modus ponens*. Only a small number of new things have to be added to the apparatus we have been examining in order to handle individuals and their properties (class memberships).

    A. There are simple conventions for representing predication.

        1. Properties that things have are represented by capital letters. Greek, wise, and mortal might be represented by G, W, and M, for example.

        2. Property holders are represented with lower case letters. Plato, Socrates, and Aristotle might be represented by p, s, and a, for example.

        3. The assertion that a property holder has a property is represented by placing a lowercase letter immediately to the right of a capital letter. Thus, "Socrates is a philosopher" might be represented Ps, "Alcibiades was a politician" might be represented Pa, and "Buchephelus was a horse" might be represented Hb.

4. Variables can function as place markers for property holders and their properties, typically lowercase Roman letters, such as **x** and **y**, etc., for the property holders and capital Greek letters, such as Φ (phi) and Ψ (psi), etc., for the properties.

B. There are two new symbols to represent the *quantity* of a proposition.

    1. **(x)**, called the *universal quantifier*, expresses the quantity of universal propositions: **(x)Φx** says that every individual has the property Φ—*everything Phis*, and **(x)~Φx** says that no individual has it—*nothing Phis.*

    2. **(∃x)**, called the *particular* (or *existential*) *quantifier*, expresses the quantity of particular propositions: **(∃x)Φx** says that at least one individual has the property Φ—*something Phis*, and **(∃x)~Φx** says that at least one individual does not—*something doesn't Phi.*

    3. In all instances, the universal or particular quantifier binds (applies to) the subsequent instances of the same variable in the same line, as guided by parentheses and other punctuation.

C. The interpretation of A and E propositions is strictly Boolean—universal statements do not assert the existence of any members of the subject class at all.

    1. Using our convention of capital Greek letters, we would write **(x)(Φx ⊃ Ψx)**: for any X, if X Phis, then X Psis. However, it may be clearer at the beginning to use S and P for subject and predicate.

    2. "All S are P" is read: *The intersection of S and ~P is null.* Using the universal quantifier, we write **(x)(Sx ⊃ Px)**: *For every individual, if it is S, then it is P.*

    3. "No S are P" is read: *The intersection of S and P is null.* Using the universal quantifier, we write **(x)(Sx ⊃ ~Px)**: *For every individual, if it is S, then it is ~P.*

    4. "Some S are P" is read: *The intersection of S and P is not null.* Using the particular quantifier, we write **(∃x)(Sx • Px)**: *There is at least one S that is P.*

    5. "Some S are not P" is read: *The intersection of S and ~P is not null.* Using the particular quantifier, we write **(∃x)(Sx • ~Px)**: *There is at least one S that is ~P.*

6. This recognizes the contradictory relationship of universal affirmatives and particular negatives, and of universal negatives and particular affirmatives. Using quantifiers, we express these relationships as equivalence statements and establish them as replacement rules (called *quantifier negation*):

~(x)Φx ≡ (∃x)~Φx:	~(x)~Φx ≡ (∃x)Φx:
It is not the case that everything Phis if and only if at least one thing does not.	*It is not the case that nothing Phis if and only if at least one thing does.*

D. Two new inference rules for instantiation (also known as *stripping quantifiers*) allow the application of general claims to individuals.

1. *Universal instantiation.* If everything possesses a property, then that property is possessed by any individual thing we choose.

Using the universal quantifier, we write:

(x)Φx   /∴ Φv (with no restrictions).

If everything phis, then nu phis— the lowercase Greek letter nu representing the name of any individual whatever.

2. *Existential (particular) instantiation.* If at least one thing possesses a property, then that one thing may be given an arbitrary name.

Using the particular quantifier, we write:

(∃x)Φx   /∴ Φv (with restrictions).

If at least one thing phis, then nu phis—the lowercase Greek letter nu representing any arbitrary name that has no prior use in the context.

III. With these additions in hand, predicate arguments can be proven utilizing all of the power of the apparatus for handling sentential arguments. For example:

All Greeks are mortals.	**(x)(Gx ⊃ Mx)**
All Athenians are Greeks.	**(x)(Ax ⊃ Gx)**
Therefore, All Athenians are mortals.	/∴ **(x)(Ax ⊃ Mx)**

1. **(x)(Gx ⊃ Mx)**   [for any x whatever, if x is Greek, then x is mortal]

2. **(x)(Ax ⊃ Gx)**   [for any x whatever, if x is Athenian, then x is Greek]

3. /∴ **(x)(Ax ⊃ Mx)** [for any x whatever, if x is Athenian, then x is mortal]

→ 4.	~(x)(Ax ⊃ Mx)	Hypothesis
5.	(∃x)~(Ax ⊃ Mx)	3 Quantifier Negation
6.	~(Aa ⊃ Ma)	4 Existential Instant.
7.	Ga ⊃ Ma	1 Universal Instant.
8.	Aa ⊃ Ga	2 Universal Instant.
9.	Aa ⊃ Ma	7, 6 Hyp. Syllogism
10.	(Aa ⊃ Ma) • ~(Aa ⊃ Ma)	8, 5 Conjunction

11. ~(x)(Ax ⊃ Mx) > [(Aa ⊃ Ma) • ~(Aa ⊃ Ma)]3–9 Conditional Proof

12. (x)(Ax ⊃ Mx)   10 Reductio

IV. With this apparatus, it is also possible to prove predicate arguments beyond the scope of Aristotelian syllogistic.

   A. Arguments with more than three terms, or with complex terms, are easy.

     Example:

     Any problem with more than three terms violates Aristotelian rules.

     This very problem has more than three terms and is demonstrably valid.

     If at least one argument is demonstrably valid and violates Aristotelian rules, then Aristotelian logic is inadequate.

     Therefore, Aristotelian logic is inadequate.

   B. With the addition of a few further conventions and rules, relational arguments can also be solved.

     Example:

     Everybody loves somebody sometime.

     I am somebody.

     Therefore, someday, there will be someone for me to love.

   C. The apparatus of modern logic is large, growing, and dynamic. It is not the easiest thing in the world to learn, but with a little application and a little focus, you can learn it, and you will have in hand the essential rational tool. The applications, which include switching circuits and a binary mathematical apparatus on which to base computer languages, are astounding.

Essential Reading:

James Hall, *Logic Problems for Drill and Review*, Chapter 1, "The Apparatus," pp. 16–20.

Recommended Reading:

Irving Copi, *Introduction to Logic,* Chapter 10, "Quantification Theory," pp. 385–413.

Questions to Consider:

1. Not all quantified arguments are valid. How could we prove a quantified argument to be invalid without constructing a truth table of infinite size? After you have thought about this question, look at page 21 in my *Logic Problems* and pages 406–408 in Copi's *Introduction.*

2. How different would a logic system have to be to accommodate statements that can have three "states" (say, *true*, *false* and *maybe*)? What would replace the law of excluded middle in such a system?

Lecture Twenty-Two
Modern Logic—Predicate Arguments

The arguments that we were looking at last time are called *sentential arguments*. They are arguments where everything depends upon the connections between simple sentences joined with such connectors as, "as," "and," "or," and "if then." Modern logic handles sentential problems very, very nicely. But modern logic also handles another kind of argument, one with which you are already familiar from our discussions of the Aristotelian syllogism many, many lectures ago. These are called *predicate arguments*, and in predicate arguments, in distinction from sentential ones, in predicate arguments everything depends upon the relationship between the subject and predicate terms within a sentence. Modern logic has the significant advantage of using one apparatus to handle both sentential and predicate arguments alike.

In order to work with predicate arguments in modern style, there are a few conventions that we are going to adopt and work with, and let me mention a few of them and get them in place very, very quickly. We are going to represent properties with capital letters—a single capital letter representing a property. We are going to represent things that have properties, *property holders* I will call them; we are going to represent them with a lower-case letter. So we have capital letters for properties and lower-case letters for the things that have them. And when we want to say that a particular individual property holder has a particular property, we will, as is shown in the first graphic in your workbook or on the screen, we will write the property letter and then immediately follow it by the property-holder letter. So, capital "P," little "s," might mean—might represent—something like Socrates is a philosopher; the property of being a philosopher being held by Socrates, the individual. Okay?

Now, obviously you could abbreviate in this way countless predicate statements. Socrates is a philosopher, Alcibiades was a politician, Bucephelus was a horse—little letters for the property holder, capital letters for the property—but it very quickly becomes useful to have variables that we can use to represent different properties and different individuals. We will follow the convention of using capital letters from the Greek alphabet as property variables, place markers for the properties that things might have, and use lower-case letters from the Roman alphabet—typically x, y, z, down towards that end of the list—for things that have the properties in question. So, we can not only talk about specifics—Socrates has the specific property of being a philosopher—we can also talk about whether or not X Phis, or Y Psis, or Z Phis, and so on. Variables are simply place markers to make our lives a little easier.

We are going to have to introduce two new symbols in order to handle predicate logic in the modern apparatus. The symbols are called *quantifiers*, and they are ways of expressing the quantity of a general predicate statement. There are two of them. There is the *universal quantifier*, which is a little x with parentheses around it, and there is the *particular quantifier*, which is for reasons no one knows, a backwards capital E with a little x following it with parentheses around it. And we read these, the universal, for all x or the particular for some x—for all x or some x. So, if I wanted to say, for instance, that everything in the universe has the property Phi, I could write for all X, Phi X. All X's Phi. Or if I wanted to say that there is at least one thing, something in the universe, that has that property, I can use the particular quantifier and write for some X, X Phi. With those conventions in place, we are in a position to represent our old, familiar standard form categorical or predicate propositions in a new symbolic dress.

I hope that you remember the A, E, I, and O propositions. The A proposition, all S's are P's; the E proposition, no S's are P's; the I proposition, some S's are P's; and the O proposition, some S's are not P's. And here, just for convenience sake, I am using S and P to represent subject and predicate in an English sentence. So, for our first A proposition, it might be all men are mortal; it might be all cocker-spaniels are dogs; it might mean all Mondays are depressing; it could be any number of different things for any X; if X is an S, then X is a P. All S's, P. Using our convention that I was just mentioning a moment ago of capital Greek letters, we would undoubtedly write for any X, if X Phis, then X Psis, but I thought it might be clearer right at the beginning to use S and P for subject and predicate.

So, all S's are P's for any X whatever. If it's an S, then it's a P. No S's are P's for an X whatever. If it's an S, then it's not a P. Some S's are P's; there is at least one X such that it is both S and P. Some S's are not P's. There is at least one X, such that it is an S, but is not a P. Something to notice that is very, very important are the universal statements, the A and the E as we are representing them, because they are symbolized with a horseshoe and are very, very clearly hypothetical. They do not exert the existence of any individual members to the subject class. You will remember our discussion of null classes. You may remember the example that I used about all of my daughters being beautiful—this being true simply because I have no daughters. But for any X whatever, if it were a daughter of mine, then it would be beautiful, no doubt. That is to say, that in the modern logical representation of general statements, we are following a Boolean interpretation in which universal statements do not assert the existence of any members of the subject class at all, where the particular affirmative and particular negative are down at the bottom, they do. They flat out say there is at least one X such that it has these properties.

Because of that Boolean interpretation being packed into the way we represent the statements, we preserve perfectly, in the new apparatus, the relationship of contradictoriness that we talked about back when we were talking about the square of opposition many, many sessions ago: that the denial of a universal affirmative is its contradictory, a particular negative; and that the denial of a universal negative is its contradictory, i.e., a particular affirmative; but instead of putting that up on a "Square of Opposition" as we did before, we now can express this as a substitution rule. Let's look at two instances of what is called the "Rule of Quantifier Negation."

To say, it is not the case that everything Phis, it is not the case that everything Phis is exactly the same as saying there is at least one thing that doesn't Phi. The denial of that universal affirmative is the particular negative. To say, it is not the case that nothing Phis—it's not the case that for all x, x fails to Phi—is exactly the same thing as saying there is at least one X that does Phi. So the rules of quantifier negation very comfortably capture the principle of contradiction, which—as you will remember—is the important principle from that old traditional Square of Opposition—the principle that needs to be maintained if we are going to be able to run logical proofs at all.

Well, we have introduced our conventions for properties and property holders. We have introduced quantifiers so that we can represent the general quality of statements, and we have seen how we can capture our traditional universal affirmative, universal negative, particular affirmative, and particular negative sentences in this new apparatus. And finally, we have seen that the old relationship of contradictoriness survives and is preserved in a very, very important set of rules called the Rules of Quantifier Negation. We are almost ready to construct a proof of a predicate argument in modern logic, but there is one more thing that we need to deal with first.

We need to introduce a way to take a quantified statement like, for any X whatever, if X Phis then X Psi, and get the quantifiers out of the way so that we can apply the Rules of Inference that we already know, like *modus ponens*, and *disjunctive syllogism*, and *hypothetical syllogism*, and the like. So we need a rule for what is sometimes called *stripping quantifiers*—a rule for getting quantifiers out of the way, or the label that I prefer, "Rules for Instantiation." To instantiate a general statement is simply to turn from the general statement itself to an instance of it. An instantiation of a general statement is an instance of that statement. We need Instantiation Rules so that we can move from universal or particular general statements, either one, to instances of them.

You will see on your screen or in your study guide, Instantiation Rules for universals and particulars, and let me talk them through because in one situation they are a little tricky. The *universal instantiation* says this: It says that if you know as a premise that everything Phis—if that is given to you as a premise, everything in the universe Phis—you are allowed to infer that *nu* Phis, that's a lower case Greek *nu*; it's the only time we use this letter, and we use it because it represents name, new name. If everything Phis, you are allowed to infer the *nu* Phis with no restrictions—that is, *nu* can be the name of any individual you'd like; if everything Phis then *nu* Phis with no restrictions.

Why am I not putting this on a truth table to establish it for you? Because, dear friends, the truth table would have to be infinitely large. The truth table would have to have a separate column for every name of every thing—every star, every planet, every grain of sand at Virginia Beach, every silicon atom in every grain of sand, and so on, and on and on. We cannot do that, but we can—at an intuitive level—very readily understand the legitimacy of this move, for if we could find any one individual that did not Phi, some new thing that did not have this property, that would be knockdown proof right there that the premise was false because the premise says everything has the property. And there is no way for everything to have it unless each individual thing has it. So, we say, intuitively, and without a truth table, that when we know that everything Phis, we may infer that *nu* Phis without restrictions.

Particulars. Suppose we only know that there is at least one thing that Phis, something Phis. How do we get that quantifier out of the way? How do we find an instance of that? Well, the rule says that we may infer from something Phis to *nu* Phis, but with restrictions in red and put an explanation mark because the restrictions are dreadfully important. Here is what the restrictions amount to. If you know that something Phis, you may name that thing with a name, *nu*, provided that that name that you choose is unique and arbitrarily chosen and has no previous occurrence in the context in which you are working, whatever. If I know that there is a Latvian lothario in the world, there is at least one Latvian lothario, I cannot—this is just among us—I cannot say "Ah ha, I am going to call him Andreas, because Andreas is an individual that we all know in our community, and we don't know whether he is a Latvian lothario or not." So, I can't go from "There is at least one thing with a certain property" to "Ah, ha, you are the one." I have to say, if there is something that has a property, I have to say let's call it—and then pick an arbitrary name that is absolutely clean.

This becomes especially important if an argument has more than one particular premise in it, because if we are trying to instantiate two particular premises, this restriction will absolutely prevent us from instantiating them both to the same individual. This is why I cannot argue that some mammals are cats and some mammals are dogs— therefore, some cats are dogs. Because I can instantiate the premise about cats to one arbitrary name, I would have to instantiate the premise about dogs to a different arbitrary name, and I would never be able to put the two together with any constructive results.

Okay, with these conventions, rules, symbols, in place, let's look at an argument. The argument I am going to look at with you is one that is very simple. You are going to say why in the world would we want to do all of the work that would be involved in really learning modern symbolic logic in order to do the argument that I am about to put up on the screen? Because it is an argument that we have done before with Venn diagrams, and it's a lot easier than what this looks like. Here is the argument: All Greeks are mortals; all Athenians are Greeks; therefore, all Athenians are mortals. That problem would have given Aristotle no problem whatever. It would have given early modern logicians with Venn diagrams no problem whatever. What I want to show you, line by line, is how we would handle this problem in the modern apparatus, and then tell you why the modern apparatus is important. And perhaps you already suspect why, it is because we are not limited to nice, neat, simple little syllogisms like this; we can unleash this apparatus on arguments of enormous complexity.

All Greeks are mortal. It gets symbolized on the first line as for any X whatever, if X is Greek, then X is mortal. All Athenians are Greek; that gets symbolized on the second line as for any X whatever; if X is an Athenian, then X is Greek. The conclusion is, therefore, all Athenians are mortals; for any X whatever, if X is Athenian, then X is mortal. For my proof technique, I am going to, in this instance— there are other ways to do it—but in this instance, I am going to use a very, very common and powerful proof technique. I am going to run a *conditional proof.* I am going to use a hypothesis and look at what I am hypothesizing. I am hypothesizing it is not the case that for all X, if X is Athenian, then X is mortal. I am hypothesizing the denial of the conclusion that I want to establish, and if that makes you think of Euclid, you get an extra bonus ten points because that is exactly the Euclidian technique. I will begin my proof by hypothesizing that the conclusion is false. I do that simply by writing the conclusion with a negation sign in front of it, labeling it hypothesis, and putting a bent arrow to the left that is going to show how far that hypothesis runs. On the very next line, line 4, I use my Rule of Quantifier Negation to get the negation sign that line 3 starts with out of the way. We haven't discussed this, just accept it if you will. You cannot instantiate a quantified line that starts with a negation sign. You have to get that negation sign out of the way— then you can use your Instantiation Rules.

So the very next thing I do is appeal to quantifier negation. I move the negation sign from the left-hand side of for some X, from the left-hand sign over from all X, over to the right-hand side, and when I do, as you saw on the specifications of the rule, the quantifier itself changes. *Not all* becomes *some not.* So on line 4, I now have, there is at least one X such that it is not the case that if it is an A, then it is an M, quantifier negation from three. I then instantiate that. I get the quantifier out of the way, and I'm saying, lets instantiate it to A, an arbitrarily selected name with no prior use, Alpha Ron. So, it is not the case that if Alpha Ron is an Athenian, then Alpha Ron is mortal.

I then instantiate the two universal premises, premise one and premise two, and remember that on universal instantiation, there were no restrictions at all. I can instantiate them to any individual whatever—so I instantiate them to Alpha Ron.

So, now, on line five, I have it is not the case that if Alpha Ron is an Athenian, then Alpha Ron is a mortal; on six, if Alpha Ron is Greek, then Alpha Ron is mortal; and on seven, if Alpha Ron is Athenian, then Alpha Ron is Greek. Now I am ready to move. On line eight, I do a hypothetical syllogism from seven and six. AA implies GA on line seven; GA implies MA on line six. That is a chain argument it goes through. I have AA implies MA on line eight, from lines seven and six, hypothetical syllogism, solid as a rock. That came from the two premises, ultimately.

But look at what I have got back up on line five. On line five, I have it is not the case that AA implies MA. That is what I got from the hypothesis after I cleared out the negation sign and then instantiated it. And what is on line five is the flat denial, the flat contradiction, of what is on line eight. So, I put those two statements together on line nine by the "Rule of Conjunction," which we have seen, and I write, A does imply M, and it's not the case that A implies M. At that point, I close off my hypothesis because I've gotten where I want to get; because I have shown that if you hypothesize that that conclusion is false, it delivers an explicit contradiction right into your lap. And so, I close off the hypothesis after line nine, and I write, if you hypothesize that it's not the case that for all X, if AX then MX, then it follows both that if AA's then it M's, and it's not the case that if AA's, then it M's. The hypothesis implies a contradiction, and that is from lines three through nine by conditional proof.

So, all that is left to do is appeal to the *Reductio Rule* because we know that at the simplest of levels, that if P implies a contradiction, P is false. This hypothesis implies a contradiction. We have demonstrated it. The hypothesis is false, and we are home clear, and we have shown—beyond a shadow of a doubt in a completely mechanical way—that from these premises, you may reach that conclusion with ease.

Now, with this apparatus—and this is very, very important—it is also possible to prove predicate arguments that go far, far beyond the scope of the Aristotelian apparatus as represented by this argument about Greeks, and mortals, and Athenians. Here is an argument: Any problem with more than three terms violates Aristotelian Rules, premise one. This very problem has more than three terms and is demonstrably valid; that is premise two. Three, if at least one argument is demonstratively valid and violates Aristotelian Rules, then Aristotelian logic is inadequate for modern purposes—therefore, Aristotelian logic is inadequate for modern purposes, and indeed, it is.

The point I am trying to make is that in the Aristotelian syllogistic, we were limited. We were confined to arguments that had only three terms. We were not able to deal with relational predicates of any kind whatever. We were straight-jacketed in astounding ways.

Let me give you another argument. I like this one: Everybody loves somebody sometime. There is a premise. I am somebody—therefore, some day there will be someone for me to love. Everybody loves somebody sometime; I am somebody—therefore, some day there will be someone for me to love. An aside: I would like to think that that argument is not only valid, but that it is sound. That would make me feel secure, and indeed, I have already found someone.

But note: There are relational matters going on in here. Everybody loves somebody sometime. We are going to have to quantify over the person who is doing the loving; we are going to have to quantify over the person who is loved; we are going to have to quantify over time. So, for any X whatever, there exists a Y, and there exists a Z—such that if X is a person, then Y is a person, and then Z is a time; then X loves Y at Z.

I am not trying to be flashy. I am just trying to make the point that a very straightforward argument about relations—which is absolutely impossible to handle in Aristotelian terms—is readily handle-able using the apparatus that we have just barely introduced.

Now, let me loop back to the beginning and reiterate something that I said at the very beginning of this introduction to modern logic. I have barely scratched the surface. There is a large, and growing, and dynamic apparatus that I would encourage you to involve yourself in and learn something about. The applications of it are astounding. We have been talking about some applications to the English language, working with things that are true and things that are false. Substitute

"On" and "Off" for "True" and "False," and we can use the same apparatus to analyze and construct better switching circuits. Or, over in the computer world, substitute zeros and ones for the "On" and the "Off" in the transistor, or the "True" or the "False," and you have got a perfectly straightforward binary mathematical apparatus on which to base computer languages, and that is where they are based.

So, the logic that we are talking about here is a treasure trove of potential applications. It is not the easiest thing in the world to learn, but with a little application and a little focus, you can learn it, and you will have in-hand the essential rational tool that is so crucial to modern *Rational Empiricism*. Remember, after all, I never said we were going to talk about just empiricism. We are talking about Rational Empiricism, and Rational Empiricists have to have the apparatus of logic in-hand in order to do their work.

Lecture Twenty-Three
Postmodern and New-Age Problems

Scope:

Modern rational empiricism is not problem-free. For instance, we know that observations themselves are *theory laden*. That means, at the least, that all our experiences are *construals* made in terms of whatever ideas and theories are already "in place" for us. This amounts to *epistemic* relativism. Further, if the general (or scientific) culture determines what those ideas and theories are, then even our simplest descriptions are *culturally* relative. These central themes of what is now called *postmodernism* were in play under the rubric "the sociology of knowledge" long before the mid-century talk of *language games*, *paradigm shifts*, and *scientific revolutions*. Epistemic and cultural relativism are also central themes of many "New Age" and religious objections to rational empiricism. Along with such issues of *relativism*, there are also issues about *uncertainty* and the possibility of *universal error*. Radical skepticism can be propagated from all of these roots.

Outline

I. Modern rational empiricism is not problem-free.

    A. Observations themselves are *theory laden*, as well as being colored by other observations that we have already made and categorized.

        1. An observation is shaped by the theories that we hold and have in use when it is made. You don't observe gravity until you have a theory of gravity in place.

        2. An observation is shaped by other observations we have already made and categorized. You can only *observe* food on the banana tree if you have some experience indicating that what grows on banana trees can be eaten.

        3. Thus, all our observations are epistemically relative *construals*, made from the perspective of whatever ideas, theories, and hypotheses are already "in place" for us.

        4. This says that we only see what we are *conceptually equipped* to see. It is why a city slicker can starve in a forest full of food and why most of what occurs on *The Simpsons* goes over the head of a four-year-old.

B. If the general (or scientific) culture determines what ideas and theories are in place for an observer, then even the simplest descriptions are also *culturally relative*.

1. This is a main theme of *postmodernism*, which has several roots.

  a. Karl Mannheim espoused "the sociology of knowledge" in the 1920s (in *Ideologie und Utopie*), arguing that all knowledge is a product of culture.

  b. Ludwig Wittgenstein talked a great deal about language games in his *Philosophical Investigations*, published in 1953 (though in circulation before that) and insisted that there were different language games that reflected different "forms of life."

  c. In the 1960s, Thomas Kuhn's notions of paradigm shifts and scientific revolutions in *The Structure of Scientific Revolutions* were based on the idea that our very scientific descriptions of what is going on in the world are the product of the favored ideas of those who are in positions of privilege and power within a particular culture at a particular time.

2. It is very easy to take this epistemic relativism so seriously as to think that we cannot reach any kind of conclusions about anything at all.

  a. Yet considering whether to dig a latrine uphill or downhill from your water source suggests that some facts are available to all of us (about infant mortality, a contaminated water supply, etc.), that can be rendered intelligible to anyone, and that are commensurable and translatable enough for people to learn very quickly that if they change their cultural tradition of where to dig their latrines, they can alter the infant mortality rate in their community.

  b. Epistemic and cultural relativism are also central themes of "New Age" and religious objections to rational empiricism.

II. Along with epistemic and cultural *relativism*, issues about *uncertainty* and the possibility of *universal error* are also problematic for rational empiricists, in that they seem to imply *radical skepticism*.

    A. *Uncertainty*: Descartes claimed that one cannot know anything that can be doubted.

    B. *Universal error*: Peter Unger has argued that we could be mistaken all the time.

    C. *Radical skepticism*: The notion is that we never know anything at all.

III. While radical skepticism can be propagated from such ideas as cultural relativism and claims and arguments such as those of Descartes and Unger, it need not be terminal.

    A. Cultural relativism denies the possibility of internal and external culture critique that actually occurs.

    B. The uncertainty argument defeats itself by equivocating over the word *certain*.

    C. The universal error argument ignores the idea that making a mistake is always parasitic on getting *something* right. Example: "All money is counterfeit."

    D. Consequently, while radical skepticism can make us reflect on how to avoid mistakes, it should not prevent us from moving forward.

    E. Once you realize that while you don't get logical certainty about matters of fact, you can get practical reliability, the threats to modern rational empiricism are effective disarmed.

Essential Reading:

Christopher Butler, *Postmodernism—A Very Short Introduction.*

Recommended Reading:

James Hall, *Practically Profound*, Chapter 7, "Knowledge and Cultural Relativism."

Questions to Consider:

1. If claims made in different paradigms are mutually "incommensurable and untranslatable," does it follow that in

olden times, the Sun really did revolve around the Earth, even though the Earth now revolves around the Sun?

2. If reality is a "text" that is "open to interpretation," does it follow that any interpretation of it is just as good as any other, any more than that any interpretation of *Hamlet* is just as good as any other?

Lecture Twenty-Three
Postmodern and New-Age Problems

We have been talking for any number of sessions now about the tools of thinking, and I have been arguing gently in favor of a position that I have been calling "modern rational empiricism." I have been trying to show you what some of the strengths are of that approach to problem solving—whether it is imbibed in the formal sciences, or whether it's imbibed in the word of a police detective, or whether it is imbibed in the work of you or me in trying to simply work our way through life; reason our from A to B without stumbling and falling in a hole somewhere along the way. But I would not want to leave you with the impression that modern rational empiricism is problem-free. Indeed, there are some significant problems or difficulties that attach to this approach to problem-solving, and today I want to look at some of those difficulties and see if we can defuse a few of them, and at least understand where they are coming from and what their implications are. That is, let's look at the problems of rational empiricism from a good, rational empiricist point-of-view. Let's unpack it and see what is going on.

First of all, everything that we do as rational empiricists ties in—in one way or another, sooner or later, genetically or confirmationally—to what we observe. We are talking about a kind of empiricism after all. The experiential link is crucial. But, it has been said frequently enough in recent years that our observations themselves are *theory laden*—that they are colored by, and shaped by, and influenced by, the theories and the conceptual apparatus and the other observations that are already "in place," all of those things that we bring with us to the experiential situation. So, an observation is shaped by the theories that we hold and that we have in use when we are making the observation itself. Well, yes, I'll agree, that is true. One does not observe gravity unless, and until, one has the concept of gravity firmly, conceptually, and logically in place. Once we have the concept of gravity in place, we then begin to observe the world differently. And things that we have observed as being somewhat random or erratic are suddenly reduced to a kind of order—an order that we bring to the situation in that conceptual apparatus that now includes Newton's law of universal gravitation.

An observation is almost inevitably going to be shaped or influenced by other observations that we have already made.

Let's look at this at a very down-home kind of level. I would insist that you cannot *observe* edible things on banana trees unless you have already had some experience that would lead you to construe what you see on banana trees as safe and nourishing. This is why a city slicker who is lost in the forest can starve to death because he does not observe what is out there as food. He does not have the requisite experience and background to categorize things in useful ways, and to see that, indeed, he is surrounded by edible, useful material. Now, this can get a little tricky. I have often wondered about that individual somewhere back in history some time, I don't know his name, who was so desperately hungry, who was so absolutely back against the wall of starvation, that he looked at an oyster for the first time and said, mmm, I am going to eat that. Now, to those of us for whom oysters are part of our everyday perceptions—and I spent my early childhood in New Orleans and was exposed to oysters at a very early age; a gunny sack full for a dollar; that shows you how old I am—oysters are just part of the furniture of the world; wonderful, wonderful things to eat. But think about that man who looked at the first one. It doesn't look nourishing. It doesn't even look very appealing when it comes right down to it. Or think about the first people who tried eating tapioca. My mother used to feed me tapioca pudding when I was a child, when I discovered that tapioca in its natural condition is deadly poison. It has to go through repeated preparatory treatments before that plant material can finally be rendered edible. And so I convinced my mother that there was the slim chance that at the processing plant they might have overlooked one or another of those stages of preparation and maybe she was putting something on the table for us children that was going to dispatch us from this world of sorrow and sin. She kept putting it on the table. It didn't do a bit of good. My argument didn't help a bit. But, it takes a certain understanding to look at the tapioca root and see it as nourishing, or an oyster, or a banana on a tree.

Our experiences, then, are not just our sensations. They are not just the twinges and the tweaks at the ends of our nerves. Our experiences, our observations, are the way that we construe the sensations that we have, and the way that we construe them is a product of all of the experiences that we have had previously, and of a great many other things as well. So, one could claim, then—and many people have claimed—that our observations are relative to the conceptual apparatus, and the prior experience, and all of the other things that come into play, that enable us to construe our sensations the way we do and arrive at the observations that we arrive at.

Another way to illustrate this is by noting the way in which a young child and an adult can sit side by side and watch *The Simpsons* on television and react to it at completely different levels of conceptualization and understanding. There is broad slapstick comedy going on for the little ones, and there is subtle wordplay going on for the adults, and it is a fascinating mixture, I'm sure designed the way it has been produced for precisely that reason—so that it can be accessed at different levels of intellectual understanding and appreciation. And my hat is off to the people who are clever enough to do that.

Now, we have known for a long time, or we have believed for a long time, that this business about *relativism* was true of values. And it is almost a cliché in our culture to say things like, "When in Rome, do as the Romans do." *De gustibus non disputandum est*—there is no arguing about taste, different strokes for different folks, whatever floats your boat, and so on, and so on, and so on. In normative and evaluative areas, we are well-familiar with the notion that everything is relative to our perspective, and our background, and our culture, and our setting, and so on, and so on. The bite, however, for modern rational empiricism is that people in the post-modern era and in the "New Age" are saying that that same relativism washes over into scientific inquiry itself—that it is not just a matter of our cultural values being a product of our other experiences and the theories that we bring with us and our way of looking at things, but even science, even medicine, even weather forecasting—that it is all somehow tied into a set of concepts that are different for different people in different cultures.

Now, there are a bunch of roots behind that post-modern view. One of them is in the work of Karl Manheim who published a very, very interesting book entitled *The Sociology of Knowledge* back in the 1920s. Manheim was arguing 85 years ago, give or take; he was arguing that all knowledge is a product of culture. And if you understand knowledge to be justified through belief, what works out from that is the notion that some things are true in one culture, and other different things are true in other cultures. And so we talk about what is knowledge for me, and what is knowledge for you, or what is knowledge for them, and it does not wash beyond the boundaries, the sociological units in which we live.

You don't have to look far in contemporary literature to see the flavor of Manheim's notion of "the sociology of knowledge" everywhere you turn. When we talk about multi-centralism and diversity—and please don't misunderstand me, I am not trying to criticize or put down multi-culturalism and diversity—but when we talk about that a significant part of the conceptual roots of that take on the world, it goes straight back to Manheim. So what is known in culture A and what is known in culture B may be radically disparate—may not connect at all.

There are also roots behind this post-modern view to the work of Ludwig Wittgenstein, particularly his work in the *Philosophical Investigations*, which were published at mid-century along about 1952-53. They were in circulation before that, but they didn't see print until about that time. Wittgenstein talked a great deal about what he called *language games* and insisted that there were different language games that reflected different—what he called—"forms of life," and that a form of life would be indigenous to a particular culture, to a particular time, and there might be no mesh between what is being articulated in one language game and one form of life with what is being articulated in some other language game and some other form of life. They might go right past one another. Wittgenstein rather famously stated at one time in the *Philosophical Investigations* that when we confront an alien form of life—when we confront the claims that are being made in that form of life—all we can say is, "This game is played. This game is played." We can't say, "You people are wrong." And, of course, they can't say, "Us people are wrong either." It is just separate forms of life running down different channels in different directions to different ends and different purposes.

Now, Thomas Kuhn in *The Structure of Scientific Revolutions* brought that home for the scientific community when he said our very scientific descriptions of what is going on in the world are the product of our culture—the product of cultural inertia, the product of the favored ideas of those who are in positions of privilege and power within a particular culture at a particular time. Well, you take Kuhn's ideas about paradigms and how they work, and Wittgenstein's ideas about different forms of life and how they fail to mesh, and you begin to work those together, and Kuhn had read Wittgenstein, believe me. Kuhn takes it to the point of saying that what is articulated in two different paradigms—Wittgenstein's two different forms of life—what is articulated in two different paradigms is mutually "incommensurable and untranslatable." We can't lay what is being said here up against what is being said here and make any corresponding comparisons at all. It does not compute. We cannot translate from, let's say, the claims made in traditional medicine in China into the claims made that would be readily understandable at the National Institutes of Health up the road. These are two different enterprises and two different worlds talking about two different things in two different ways—mutually incommensurable, mutually untranslatable—and it's all perfectly okay. All we can say is, "This game is played."

There is no privilege in the post-modern era that is going to be attached to any particular way of looking at the world. No way of looking at the world is privileged over any other way of looking at the world. You might want to say, you might think, "Well, couldn't we put claims that are made in these different forms of life, couldn't we put them to work, and couldn't we see which ones work? And couldn't maybe one of these games be found to be wanting?" And Wittgenstein's point, and Kuhn's point, and everybody else's point is that you can't do that from outside. If there is going to be any weighing of the claims that are made within the culture of traditional medicine, those evaluations, and those checks, and that testing is going to have to be done within the apparatus and within the rules of traditional medicine. Incommensurable, untranslatable.

Now, quite frankly, I find this troubling, and I think that it is very, very easy to take this—I am going to call it *epistemic* relativism along with the *normative* relativism of an earlier age—to take this epistemic relativism so seriously as to think that we really cannot reach any kind of conclusions about anything at all; as to come to the conclusion, if you please, that there really are not any hard and fast facts out there, or at least not any that we have any access to in terms of which we could verify, or confirm, or disconfirm whatever set of attitudes, and beliefs, and so on that we bring to bear on the world around us. And if we do that, I think we are opening ourselves up to catastrophically tragic results.

I had students years ago who went to a certain part of the world as part of the Peace Corps, to help the people who lived in that part of the world learn to do some very, very simple matters having to do with hygiene. One of the things that they were doing was teaching people in that part of the world how to dig latrines. And one of the important things that they were teaching, which ran absolutely counter to the local traditions, was that when you dig a latrine, you really, really need to dig it well downhill from your source of drinking water. You dig the latrine downhill from the well—not uphill from the well. I don't need to draw you diagrams. It has to do with the direction of water flow; it has to do with typhoid; it has to do with the propagation of parasites in the water supply; and it has to do with alarmingly high levels of infant mortality.

I would want to argue that there are some facts—call them what you will; understand it in terms of traditional medicine; understand it in terms of germ theory; understand it any way you would like—there are some facts that are available to all of us about infant mortality, and water supply, and contaminated water supply, etc., that can be rendered intelligible to anyone, commensurable and translatable enough for people to understand what is being said, and for people to learn very, very quickly that if they change their cultural tradition of where they dig their latrines and where they dig their wells, they can alter the infant mortality rate in the community. And that is called *concomitant variation*, and that is part of Mill's methods of inductive reasoning, and that is part of modern rational empiricism. And I would want to argue that all the talk about incommensurability and untranslate-ability, sooner or later, comes right up face-to-face with the intractability of the environment in which we are trying to survive. And it demands from us some recognition of the objectivity of that world out there and some responsibility to bend our theories, and change our theories, and improve our theories, to come to terms with that world more adequately.

Along with cultural epistemic relativism, there are some other problems for modern rational empiricists, and some of these are very old. They have been around a long time. There are problems about *uncertainty*. There are problems about the possibility of *universal error*—problems that seem to lead, if you take them seriously, directly towards what has been called, in the tradition, *radical skepticism*—directly towards the notion that, well, we don't really know anything at all.

Questions about uncertainty are as old as Descartes, whom we have talked about, and you will remember Descartes's notion that we don't know anything about which we can entertain some doubts. Anything that is doubtful is not known. But if everything can be doubted, including Descartes's *cogito ergo sum* as well, it can be as we tried to show earlier on—if everything can be doubted, and if we don't know anything that is doubtable, then it seems to follow inevitably that we don't know anything at all.

Now, what this leads to is the notion that it is all just a matter of opinion. It is just all a matter of what I happen to believe and what you happen to believe, and that at a somewhat more naive level than the post-modernists' notions, is the same thing all over again. It is a relativising of the notion of knowledge, to the point that knowledge simply is not recognized as existing at all.

Peter Unger, a contemporary philosopher, has argued in support of radical skepticism from an argument that claims the possibility of universal error. Very, very simply, the argument goes that since it is pretty clear and we can understand this at a very straightforward level, it is pretty clear that we could make a mistake or we could be making a mistake about virtually any claim under the sun. And we can readily understand how this claim might be based on an error, or a mistake, or a flaw, or that claim might be based on an error, or a mistake, or a flaw. What is to prevent the possibility that we are, in fact, basing all claims on mistakes, and errors, and flaws, and then insofar as universal error is possible, then there is nothing that is justified to true belief. There is nothing that qualifies as knowledge. There is not any knowledge at all.

But, while radical skepticism can be propagated from that kind of roots, from questions about uncertainty and questions about the possibility of universal mistakes, and so on, I think we can defuse that somewhat in the same way that I was trying to talk about defusing the post-modernist's position. I have tried to defuse the post-modernist position to a certain extent by pointing out the interrelationship that is inevitable between observers—whether they are traditional physicians, or whether they are Western allopathic physicians; whether they are rational empiricist philosophers, or whether they are shamans in some differently organized culture in the Southwest—we all have to come to terms with a common external world that is intractable; that is frequently adverse. We have to accommodate to it. We have to do everything we can to try to make it accommodate to us, and it's in that crucible of hard confrontation with brute facts that we finally learn to appreciate, I think, the pragmatic effectiveness of the rational empiricists' methodology.

Well, similarly with universal doubts and universal mistakes and all the rest of it, I don't think this is too subtle; I think this point is pretty clear. What I want to say is that the notion of making a mistake is inevitably parasitic on the notion of getting *something* right. We cannot make sense; we cannot render intelligible even the idea of being mistaken about something except in contrast to some benchmark or paradigm of getting it right. "Mistaken" is a parasitic word.

Let me illustrate it—we have got a little bit of time left—let me illustrate it in a very, very everyday kind of way. Suppose I went to the bank to get change for a twenty-dollar bill, and the person at the counter told me I can't do that, that the twenty-dollar bill is counterfeit, and, very upset, I went home, and I come back with a different twenty-dollar bill, and I get the same response. And so I say, "Well, I have got this hundred-dollar bill I have been keeping for years, and years, and years for an emergency, and I have got to have change, can you change this?" "Oh, that is counterfeit too." And I say, "Oh my goodness, what is going on? What is going on? Is there some gigantic conspiracy in my hometown that is cranking out funny money by the truckload and driving the good stuff out of circulation so that—and I ask the bank clerk, "Is there this wave of counterfeiting going on in Richmond, Virginia?" And they say, "No, no, you misunderstand me. The point I am trying to make, sir, is that there is no such thing as real money. It is all counterfeit." Well, now, hold on, wait a minute, no, that does not even make sense. There can't be counterfeit money unless there is some real stuff, or unless there has been at least—at some time—some real stuff, because what counterfeit means is not that.

Just like counterfeit is in the realm of money, parasitic on the notion of legal tender, making mistakes in the real world is parasitic on the notion of, at least once in a while, getting something right. And as soon as we have that much of our toe in the door, we can then begin to look at the arguments from the possibility of universal mistakes for what they are. They are good stories. They are highly entertaining. They make us reflect, and recalibrate, and pay serious attention because we don't want to be making mistakes all the time. But then we can move forward. Similarly with Descartes's notions about the universality of possible doubt—the impossibility of achieving certainty—the problem there was that the kind of certainty he wanted us to achieve, which is impossible, is logical certainty. But you don't get logical certainty about matters of fact. You get logical certainty about matters of logic and mathematics. About matters of fact, you get practical reliability—things that pragmatically work—and that we have got, no problem at all. And so the threats are just that—they are threats. And modern rational empiricism—hard at work, shoulder to the wheel, nose to the grindstone—keeps plowing on to mix a whole bunch of metaphors.

Lecture Twenty-Four
Rational Empiricism in the 21st Century

Scope:

For modern rational empiricists, the basic tools of thinking are experience, memory, association, pattern discernment and recognition, reason (including the dialectic of hypotheses and counterexamples), and invention and experimentation, working together to reach probable understandings of reality (with as few appeals to intuition as possible). Such tools do not yield logical certainty about matters of fact, but they do yield a network of evidence in terms of which we can pursue truth *as a limit*. Thinking, so seen, is an *open-ended* and *self-corrective* enterprise, the history of which is marked by dead ends, as well as achievements (both of which are highly instructive). The enterprise of thought is far from over. The tools of thinking are available to all. There are useful places for all of us to put them to use, if we will spend the efforts to master them.

Outline

I.   For modern rational empiricists, the basic tools of thinking are experience, memory, association, pattern discernment and recognition, reason (including dialectic and the construction of hypotheses and counterexamples), invention, and experimentation.

   A. Experience provides the basic new input for our thinking: what we see, taste, smell, feel, hear. It can be first- or secondhand. It is as reliable as tests show it to be.

   B. Memory provides a link to data previously collected by whatever means.

   C. Association functions with both immediate experience and with remembered experiences to group the data we have into clusters and sets.

   D. Pattern discernment and recognition enable us to make those clusters and sets useful.

   E. Reason (including dialectic and the construction of hypotheses and counterexamples) is the tool that we use to draw inferences from what we have observed, remembered, and associated. It takes many forms, such as deduction, generalization, extrapolation, and hypothesis construction, and may be linear or dialectical in form.

F. Invention supplies us with hypotheses, construals, models, and theories about what we observe and how it can most fruitfully be put to use.

G. Experimentation (in our heads, in the field, or in the laboratory) is the tool we use to test our hypotheses, construals, models, and theories to see how well they work and whether they need revision or replacement in order to work better.

H. Intuition is a good thing when it happens, but it is rare and (by definition) uncharted.

II. Things works best when we use these tools together to reach probable understandings of reality (with as few appeals to intuition as we can get by with).

A. Experience, memory, association, and pattern discernment and recognition, working together, supply the raw material for our inferences and explanations.

B. Reason in all its forms, along with invention and experimentation, utilizes that input, construes it, constructs possible accounts of it, and puts those accounts to the test.

C. Intuition is a label that we can use for starting points—those things that seem "basic"—and for the bolder inventive leaps that we make when they happen to succeed. It is no substitute for thought, however.

III. Such tools do not yield logical certainty about matters of fact, but they do yield a network of evidence in terms of which we can pursue truth *as a limit*.

A. Logical certainty about matters of fact is a will-o-the-wisp, but highly reliable conclusions about matters of fact are readily available to those who seek them.

B. "Truth" is a label we use for the limit toward which we perpetually strive in our thinking. It is not a label for where we happen to be at any moment in the quest. What we have achieved at any moment in the quest is, at best, an *approximation* of truth.

IV. There is a shred of truth in the claim that science, in the era of "big science," has become one more piece of the ideological give and take of a politicized world.

   A. It is very difficult to do certain kinds of research without massive funding, and funding is tied to the agendas of the federal government, of foundations, or of various philanthropic groups that provide it.

   B. But the wonderful thing about modern rational empiricism is that it can be practiced by mavericks, even when they do not have massive funding.

V. Thinking, so seen, is an *open-ended* and *self-corrective* enterprise, the history of which is marked by dead ends, as well as achievements (both of which are highly instructive).

   A. There is an infinitesimally minimal likelihood that we will ever be able to say, "Well, we don't need to think anymore; we've gotten there." Indeed, the more we think, the more things to think about we think of. It is a truly open-ended enterprise.

   B. While it is possible to hare off in our thoughts, disciplined thinking tests itself and corrects itself by putting output up against expectation, always remembering that where we are *now* is only an approximation of where we are trying to go.

   C. In the process of weighing outputs, we will often find them wanting. But this serves as a spur to further inquiry and permanently marks (for those who remember with care) paths that can be abandoned for more promising alternatives. Once we understand even the basics of biochemistry, for example, we are unlikely to fund any more expeditions to look for the fountain of youth but very likely indeed to fund medical research.

VI. The enterprise of thought is far from over. The tools of thinking are available to all. There are useful places for all of us to put them to use, if we will spend the efforts to master them.

   A. The systematic study of logic, science, mathematics, history, and even philosophy are all good places to begin.

   B. We see before us—even today—a vista, a wide-open horizon, that beckons us forward to press on with the search, to perpetually think in the best ways that we can, and to make better lives for ourselves and for those to come.

Three Books to Read Next:

Isaac Asimov, *Asimov's Chronology of Science and Discovery*.

Stephen W. Hawking, *The Illustrated Theory of Everything: The Origin and Fate of the Universe*.

Steven Pinker, *How the Mind Works*.

Questions to Consider:

1. Why should one think that the fact that scientific explanations of things have changed over time is any indication that scientific truth is an oxymoron or a poor second cousin to revealed truth?

2. When we encounter stubborn phenomena that we do not understand and cannot explain, which is better: grooving on the mystery or rolling up our sleeves and getting to work?

Lecture Twenty-Four
Rational Empiricism in the 21st Century

I suggested at the beginning of this series of lectures that the "basic" tools of thinking include experience; memory; association; pattern discernment and recognition; reason, including as part of reason, dialectic and the construction of hypotheses and counterexamples and experimental testing, invention, and experimentation. Those basic tools, I would suggest to you, are the tools that are at the heart of what I have been calling in the later part of this series, "modern rational empiricism." Let's go back and look at them one more time.

Experience provides, if you please, the basic new input for the thinking that we are going to do. It is the source of raw material for our thinking. What we see, and what we taste, and what we smell, and what we feel, and what we hear, gives us data to reflect upon; to manipulate; to hypothesize about; to explain; to try to figure out; to try to understand. We noted, and it is an important matter to note, that experience does not need to be first-hand. It is crucially important to realize that we can utilize experience second-hand, third-hand, tenth-hand. And so through the experience of what we read and of what we are told, we can access the experience of others—what they perhaps, indeed, first-hand saw and tasted and smelled and felt and heard.

A foot note: Even as I said at the beginning, I do not want to be narrow-minded about the range of things that I would allow to fall within the family of experience modes. There are controversies over exactly which modes of experience are reliable. There are those who claim to have experience via extrasensory channels. There are those who claim to have experiences of the divine, or of the transcendent. I am not dismissive toward them at all. All I want to say is that experience of whatever sort is going to be what furnishes the input with which our thinking begins, and the usefulness of that experience is going to depend upon how it survives the tests, and the trials, and vicissitudes of the thinking that we do with it. And, I will be frank to say that I think that some kinds of experience survive those tests and trials considerably better than others. But that is for, that is something for one to test out for one's self to take note of the experience that comes your way, find out which of those experiences are reliable and which are not, and move on with them productively.

Memory. Memory provides the link back to all of those experiences that were longer than just a moment ago. And if we did not have memory to tap into that storehouse of accumulated experiences in the past, we would never be in a position to move forward. For as we moved forward, we would lose everything that we had achieved thus far. We would be perpetually at the starting point—perpetually making no forward movement at all.

Association. Association functions, I think, to bring together the experiences that we have—the experiences that we remember, the data that we read about—and begin to link it into some kind of rudimentary patterns to begin to make some kind of sense or structure out of it. And that association may be habitual; it may be triggered by odd imprints that have been made on our memory in the past.

I talked earlier on about the way in which odors can trigger, by way of association, a whole family of memories associated with that odor at some earlier time. For me, the key one is the odor of baking bread and my grandparents' house in Illinois, where I spent many a happy summer in my childhood. I cannot smell bread baking in an oven without having the vista of my grandmother's kitchen open before me, and the memories come pouring back in of those happy years.

As we associate what we remember and what we sense, we begin to pick out patterns, and, perhaps, we begin to impose patterns, pattern discernment, pattern recognition, maybe even pattern imposition. But it is when we begin to cluster that information—that input—together in some pattern kind of way that it becomes useful. And we are finally in a position to begin to reason about it; reason with it; reason from it; construct hypotheses; and reason to it; to construct explanations about it. And thus, reason comes into play. We are drawing inferences from what we have observed, and what we remember, and what we associate in any number of different rational patterns. It may be as with the logic we have been looking at in recent lectures, a deductive pattern. It may be as with Mill's methods that we talked about a little longer ago in an inductive pattern. It may be with Newton, the construction of hypotheses, and then experimentally testing them out by reason; I mean all of that family of activities taken together and collectively. And there, of course, is where the hard work gets done, because there is where we have to, so-to-speak, roll up our mental sleeves and do something with the input data that we have in our hands and the things that we remember to actually move forward with them. Whether we move forward in a linear fashion, or whether we move forward in a dialectical back and forth kind of fashion, matters not at all.

Invention is a tool of thinking that, regrettably from my vantage point, is not quite as readily available to all of us as reason, and experience, and memory, and so on, are. Invention is the point at which people of genius, people of creative imagination, make leaps; suggest new ways of construing the data; out of the blue suggest a hypothesis that we can put to work and try on for size. Were it not for the inventors, were it not for the creators, there would be very little for the rest of us to do other than plow the same old ground over, and over, and over again.

But, as we are plowing that ground, and as we are trying to exploit the inventive genius of those who point us in new directions, we have to keep our reasoning under some kind of constraint. And the constraint that I am talking about is not keeping reason on a leash—it is not thinking about this, or that, or the other because that is taboo, or I'm not allowed to do this—no, no, not at all. What I am talking about is keeping our reasoning under the constraint of testing; of constantly looking to see whether what we have reasoned to is cashing out in the arena of the experiences that we are *now* having. And that, of course, is where experimentation—whether in our heads, in thought experiments, or whether in the laboratories in programs of disciplined organized experimentation—wherever and however it takes place, that experimental testing is the crucial thing to keep our thinking responsible and to keep it focused.

The one thing I haven't mentioned directly in this context this time is intuition. I like to think of intuition in this context as a nice label to put on what those bold inventive geniuses offer to us. But as I said at the beginning of the lecture series, usually by the word "intuition" we mean very little more than here is an idea, and we don't really know where it came from. I am not opposed to that. We are told in an old cliché not to look a gift horse in the mouth. If anybody offers me an intuition, I am perfectly willing to take it and run with it, subject to test—subject to the constraint that I would impose on any line of thought whatever. Things work best, I believe, when we use these tools together. When we use them together, we reach probable conclusions—probable understandings of reality.

Now, if we use intuition, or invention, or flashes of insight or creativity as one of the starting points, and if we use the common everyday experience that all of us have as another of the starting points, and if we use the accumulated record of the experiences, and understandings, and explanations of all of those who go before us— on whose shoulders we stand as another starting point—if we bring all of these things together, then experience, and memory, and association, and pattern discernment, and pattern recognition, working together, supply us with all the raw material we could conceivably want for the construction of inferences, hypotheses, explanations, theories, experimental programs to weigh them out and *as a limit*, as a target, understanding, indeed, knowledge. Reason in all of its forms—along with invention and experimentation that utilizes the input that we have, that construes that input, that constructs possible accounts of that input, and then puts all of those things to the test—that is, for most of us, where there is the most profit to be made, the most to be gained, because reasoning is something that we can learn to do and learn to do better. We can also learn to observe more closely and more carefully. I don't think we can learn to have creative insights. I tend to suspect that creative genius is innate.

Now, using those tools, what do we get? Do we get logical certainty about matters of fact? Do we get things that can be chiseled into stone and are eternal, and universal, and absolute, and unshakable? Not if we are modern rational empiricists. Well, indeed, I don't think we get it no matter what we are, but if we are modern rational empiricists, we are not looking for that kind of thing to chisel in stone forever. Quite frankly, we are not looking for it because we don't think it is in the cards. We don't think it is there to be had. What we are looking for is a sharper and sharper approximation—an increasingly improved approximation of what some such general, or absolute, or universal truth might more or less look like should it ever happen.

I have a particular model in my head that I like to use when I am thinking of this kind of thing, and it is pretty straightforward. If you do a graph, and you have a vertical axis and you have a horizontal axis, and you are graphing a curve on those two axes, you can set up your formula for the curve in such a way that as the curve moves out on the axis over each unit of its extension, it approaches the axis— reducing its distance by half. We say of such a curve on a graph that it approaches the axis as its limit. It also approaches being parallel to the axis as its other limit. The farther you go, the closer you get, but no matter how close you get, you are never there. Now, if we use that as a model, I like to think of absolute truth, or absolute knowledge, or the things that we are going to inscribe on stones, etc., that is a limit that we are striving toward. It is not something that we are ever in a position to say we have got it.

Now let me take time out from that for just a moment to illustrate it in a very concrete way. And the illustration that I am going to use is a fairly pointed one, and I wouldn't want you to misconstrue my point in using it. I want to talk for just a moment about the criticisms that are sometimes offered of science by people of a religious outlook—particularly, comments that are sometimes made about Darwinian evolution by people who are of an intelligent-design, creation-science outlook. One of the things that religious thinkers frequently say as a criticism of scientific thinking is that scientific thinking is always changing. You can look over the history of science, and what is being propounded as scientific truth in 1500 is not the same thing that is being propounded as scientific truth in 1600, or 1700, or 1800, or later—constant, constant change.

In contrast, certain religious folks say real truths are eternal, and absolute, and have been laid down, perhaps revealed by the Almighty, and are fixed and unchanging. And given a choice between the rock of ages, unchanging, and the vacillation and changeability of scientific inquiry, they are inclined to go with the solidity, and the endurance, and the permanence of that revealed truth. So, they look at scientific theories changing over time as a weakness of scientific inquiry—as a sign of scientific inquiries' ineptness, of its ultimate failure.

A modern rational empiricist, however, looks at it in a completely different way. It is that openness of scientific inquiry to change that makes it scientific, and makes it worthwhile, and makes it useful. So, Newton gave us a theory of universal gravitation that was predicated in terms of an understanding of the world as matter in motion in a completely causally determinant structure. A few centuries later, Einstein tells us, well this dividing line between matter and motion is a little bit fuzzy because matter and energy are maybe two sides of the same coin. And Heisenberg is telling us that this strict causal nexus that everything is locked into that make those Newtonian predictions possible and reliable is a little fuzzy—particularly when we are at the level of very, very small subatomic phenomenon.

And so, there is a scientific revolution, and Newtonian science is replaced by relativity theory and indeterminacy theory, and maybe we will see chaos theory, and so on, and on, and on—and yet, there is a continuity. There are links as we move through. It still makes perfectly good sense to use Newtonian science when we are talking about macro phenomenon as a straightforward sort of visible level. If we want to do high-end astronomy, we had probably better make some adjustments. If we are going to be doing subatomic stuff, we are going to need to make some other adjustments. But, it is a good approximation and one that has been improved time, and time, and time again, and probably is going to get improved again—maybe within our lifetime, maybe tomorrow, who knows?

So, what some religious thinkers see as a weakness or a shortcoming of rational empiricist methodology is, by the rational empiricists themselves, seen as the very strength and point of the methodology that they are putting forward, because they are not conceiving of truth or knowledge as some absolute prize, once-and-for–all, delivered and never to change. They are conceiving it, I believe, using my model again, *as a limit* towards which we perpetually strive. Any claim we make, then, is—at best—an *approximation* of truth. But the other half of our methodology—testing, testing, testing—sees to it that the approximations of truth that we arrive at generate new experimental situations to test them yet again—to stimulate the articulation of new hypotheses—and so genuine progress takes place.

Now, as I have intimated in the immediately previous lecture, there are those today who would suggest that this notion that science is inexorably progressive is a nice piece of self-delusion; who would suggest that science is, in fact, so driven by cultural and ideological impulses—and is so governed by the preferential ideas of those who are in positions of power and influence—that science is, in fact, no more than one more piece of the ideological give and take of a totally politicized world.

There is a shred of truth in that. In an era that has been called "the era of big science," it is very, very difficult to do certain kinds of research without massive funding. And it is very, very difficult to get the massive funding that you need to do certain kinds of research any place else but the federal government, foundations, various philanthropic groups—every one of which has an agenda and, like it or not, is going to be funding research and inquiry that is aimed at the fulfillment of whatever agenda it is that they are pushing.

Case in point—try to get substantial funding for certain kinds of stem cell research today, given the posture that the federal government has taken on those kinds of stem cell research. And yet, stem cell research is simply something that you cannot easily do, shall we say; it is not something that you could easily do in your kitchen or your garage with a little bit of spare money that you have left over at the end of the week. The instrumentation, and because of the instrumentation, the funding, the training, the assistance that you are going to need, it all depends on, being big science, it depends on big money, and big money follows the directions of those who have it. And that is true.

But the wonderful thing about modern rational empiricism is that it can be practiced by mavericks, even when they do not have massive funding—and it may well be in a particular era or at a particular time when the winds of political ideology are blowing one way rather than another; blowing to the left; blowing to the right. It may be that at a particular time, certain lines of research are not going to be pursued. But those winds change, and even when the prevailing winds are blowing in one particular direction, individuals are out there thinking, hypothesizing, doing incredible things on their own hook. So I think it is unnecessarily pessimistic to say it is all just a matter of the push of ideology; it's all politicized. I think there is still room for the radical independent mind to go to work and say, "I am going to pay close attention to my input; I am going to use the best methods that I can; I am going to use all of the creativity that is available to me to come up with hypotheses that will lead me on in new directions, and I am going to test, and test, and test, and test, and sometimes it is going to come up craps."

The history of inquiry is a history of brilliant discoveries and dead-end streets. And I want to suggest to you as one of the last points to be made, that those dead-end streets are just as important as the brilliant discoveries, because as we work methodically, we are going to use our memory to mark out those dead-end streets and close them down and move on in new directions. If we didn't, we would be condemned to try the same failed hypotheses again, and again, and again, without results. So, it is important that we keep a map of all the roads that we have tried to go down, as well as all of the pitfalls that have presented themselves to us. And, of course, it is also important because sometimes as we are reflecting back, we think, "Wait a minute, there is a way I could have worked around that road block," and we will go back and give it another lick.

So, in the process of weighing outputs in our experimentation, we will often find them wanting, but this serves to spur us to further inquiry and permanently marks off paths that we need not follow yet again. We learn from our mistakes. Once you have learned even a smidgen of biochemistry, and once the people in government have learned even a smidgen of biochemistry, it is highly unlikely—not impossible, but it is highly unlikely—that the National Institutes of Health are going to be funding any more excursions to try to find the Fountain of Youth. We know better than that, finally. So, you know, we learn from our mistakes, and it is a very good thing that we do.

Last words. The enterprise of thinking is not over, and it is never going to be over. I don't think we are ever going to get to the point where we can say, "Well, we don't need to think anymore; we have gotten there." If we did, I guess we could inscribe everything that we had arrived at in stone, and set it up, and lean back and groove on it. But I don't think the world works that way. I think we see before us, even today, a vista—a wide open horizon that beckons us forward to perpetually press on with the search; to perpetually think in the best ways that we can; to make better lives for ourselves and for those to come.

Timeline

c. –1300 .... Decimal system in use in China

c. –500 .... Early logic in India and China

–470 to –399 .... **Socrates**; Socratic dialectic introduced, sophistry refuted

–427 to –347 .... **Plato**; foundations laid for classical metaphysical idealism in such dialogues as *Republic*

–384 to –322 .... **Aristotle**; foundations laid for classical logic in the *Analytics* and for empirical investigation in *History of Animals*

–325 to –265 .... **Euclid of Alexandria**

c. –300 .... Publication of Euclid's *Elements*; Babylonian Salamis (origin of the abacus) in use; zero comes into use in Babylon and India

25 .... Christianity founded

622 .... Muslim Calendar Year 1

c. 900 .... Zero introduced in West by Arab traders

c. 1000 .... Decimal system appears in West

1066 .... Battle of Hastings

1095 .... Crusades begin

1126–1198 .... **Averroës**; preservation of Aristotelian rationalism and logic

1215 .... Magna Carta

1225–1274 .... **Thomas Aquinas**; reclaiming of Aristotelian rationalism and logic in the Christian West

1240 .... Roger Bacon reintroduces Aristotle to the University of Paris

1280–1349	**William of Ockham**; introduction of Ockham's Razor
1291	Crusades end
1473–1543	**Nicolas Copernicus**; modern rational empiricism begins to define "science"
1492	Columbus sailed the ocean blue
1519–1522	Ferdinand Magellan circumnavigates the globe
1531	Erasmus publishes first complete edition of Aristotle
1561–1626	**Francis Bacon**
1564–1642	**Galilei Galileo**; refutation of Aristotelian astronomy
1571–1630	**Johannes Kepler**
1596–1650	**René Descartes**
1609	Publication of Kepler's *Astonomica Nova*, including his first two laws of planetary motion, gives a solid foundation for the modern scientific method
1614	John Napier invents logarithms
1620	Publication of Bacon's *Novum Organum*
1633	William Oughtred invents the slide rule
1637	Publication of Descartes' *Discourse on Method*, including the introduction of analytic geometry
1642–1660	English Revolution, Civil War, and Protectorate
1642–1727	**Isaac Newton**

1643	Blaise Pascal's "Pascaline" calculating device introduced
1646–1716	**Gottfried Leibniz**
1662	Publication of *Port Royal Logic*
c. 1665	Newton and Gottfried Leibniz simultaneously invent the calculus
c. 1670	Anton van Leeuwenhoek's lenses makes microbiology possible
1674	Leibniz invents the "stepped rocker" calculating device (the basis of the Monroe Calculator of 1912)
1687	Publication of Newton's *Principia*: Newton's laws of motion, the foundation of modern physics
1698	Thomas Severy steam engine
1711–1776	**David Hume**
1712	Thomas Newcomen steam engine
1724–1804	**Immanuel Kant**
1735	Carl Linnaeus's *Systema Naturae* published (biological taxonomy)
1748	Publication of Hume's *Philosophical Essays* (aka *An Enquiry Concerning Human Understanding*)—quintessential early modern empiricism, rejection of "sophistry and illusion"
1769	James Watt's steam engine
1776–1783	American Revolution
1781	Publication of Kant's *Critique of Pure Reason*; reason and experience differentiated, the analytic/synthetic distinction triumphant; the search for the synthetic *a priori*

1789–1795	French Revolution
1798	Edward Jenner publishes report on cowpox and smallpox
1798–1857	**Auguste Comte**
1806–1871	**Augustus DeMorgan**
1806–1873	**John Stuart Mill**
1812–1814	War of 1812
1815	Waterloo
1815–1864	**George Boole**
1821	Michael Faraday's electric motor
1822	Publication of Comte's *Plan de traveaux scientifiques necessaries pour réorganiser la société*; the application of observation and experimentation to sociology (and a foundation for logical positivism in the 20th century)
1822–1895	**Louis Pasteur**
c. 1825	Charles Babbage's "Difference Engine" (developed from an idea of J. H. Miller of 1786); the idea behind computers
1830	Joseph Henry's telegraph (made commercial in 1844 by Morse)
1834–1923	**John Venn**
1835	James Woodward's and Matthew Evans's electric light bulb
1839–1914	**Charles Sanders Peirce**
1842–1910	**William James**
1847	Publication of DeMorgan's *Formal Logic*; one beginning for modern

	symbolic logic, especially DeMorgan's theorems
1847	Publication of Boole's *The Mathematical Analysis of Logic*; another beginning for modern symbolic logic, especially set theory
1848–1925	**Gottlob Frege**
1856	Charles Babbage's "Analytical Engine"
1858–1932	**Giuseppe Peano**
1858–1947	**Max Planck**
1859	Charles Darwin's *On the Origin of Species* published
1861	Ignatz Semmelweis published explanation of childbed fever; confirmed by Lister in 1865
1861–1865	American Civil War
1866	Gregor Mendel explains inheritance in peas
1872–1970	**Bertrand Russell**
1873	Publication of Peirce's "Description of a Notation for the Logic of Relatives" (the predicate logic of relations)
1878	Ramon Varea invents a partial-product calculating device (basis of the Burroughs Calculating Machine of the 1920s)
1879–1955	**Albert Einstein**
1881	Introduction of Venn diagrams
1887	Michelson-Morley experiment; aether rejected

1889	Publication of Frege's *Begriffsschrift*, an apparatus, including truth tables, for the formal analysis of logical arguments
1889	Publication of Peano's *Geometrical Calculus*, including a chapter on mathematical logic with the basics of what has become "Peano-Russell Notation" for modern logic
1889	Publication of Peano's *Arithmetices Principia*, defining natural numbers in terms of sets
1889–1951	**Ludwig Wittgenstein**
1891	Publication of Mill's *A System of Logic*, the classical formulation of inductive reasoning
1899	Guglielmo Marconi's radio telegraph
1901–1976	**Werner Heisenberg**
1902–1994	**Karl Popper**
1903	Ivan Pavlov confirms conditioned reflexes in dogs
1905	Einstein's special theory of relativity
1905	X and Y chromosomes described
1906	Mechanical television
1907	Publication of James's *Pragmatism*, notable for its influence on Bertrand Russell and Ludwig Wittgenstein
1908–2000	**W. V. O. Quine**
1910	Publication of Russell's *Principa Mathematica*, Vol. 1
1910–1989	**Alfred Jules Ayer**

1912	Publication of Russell's *Principia Mathematica*, Vol. 2
1912	Publication of James's *Essays in Radical Empiricism*
1913	Publication of Russell's *Principa Mathematica*, Vol. 3
1913	J. B. Waton's "Psychology as a Behaviorist Views It" published
1914–1918	World War I
1915	Einstein's general theory of relativity
1921	Publication of Wittgenstein's *Tractatus Logico-Philosophicus*
1922–1996	**Thomas Kuhn**
1924	J. B. Watson's *Behaviorism* published
1926	Proof of Planck's Quantum Theory by Paul Dirac
1927	Publication of Heisenberg's Uncertainty Principle
1927	Philo Farnsworth files patent for electronic television
1929	Karl Mannheim publishes *Ideologie und Utopie*, setting out the "sociology of knowledge"—the roots of postmodern epistemic relativism
1936	Publication of Ayer's *Language, Truth and Logic*, bringing logical positivism to the English-speaking world
1938	B. F. Skinner's *The Behavior of Organisms* published

1938	Otto Hahn and Fritz Strassman; first fission of uranium
1938–1945	World War II
1942	First controlled nuclear reaction (Chicago)
1945	ENIAC; computers arrive for military use
c. 1950	First nuclear fusion weapons
1951	UNIVAC; computers arrive for civilian use (Census Bureau)
1951	Publication of Quine's "Two Dogmas of Empiricism," disputing the traditional empiricists' bright-line analytic/synthetic distinction
1953	The double helix: Francis Crick and James Watson explain the molecular structure of DNA
1953	Publication of Wittgenstein's *Philosophical Investigations*
1953	Publication of Popper's *Conjectures and Refutations*, including the article "Science as Falsification," putting a different twist on the logical positivists' verificationism
1960	TIROS photos of Earth from space
1962	Publication of Kuhn's *The Structure of Scientific Revolutions*, introducing the notion of "paradigm shifts" and sharply contextualizing the notion of scientific knowledge
1963	First electronic calculating device (the Sumlock)
1971	First pocket electronic calculator

1973 ....Internet conceived and designed

1974 ....First PC kit: Altair

1977 ....First working PCs: Apple II and Tandy

1983 ....Internet rollout

1989 ....The Web

1990 ....First gene replacement therapy

Glossary

A Posteriori: Known or knowable on the basis of experience of some sort.

A Priori: Known or knowable independent of experience of any sort.

Analytic: Traditionally, the character of a statement that can be shown to be true or false by logical analysis; logically necessary. See **Synthetic**.

Analytic Falsehood: Traditionally, a statement whose predicate denies what is contained in its subject; a self-contradiction or necessary falsehood.

Analytic/Synthetic Distinction: An alleged "dogma" of empiricism (see Biographical Note for **Quine, W. V. O.**) in terms of which statements can be neatly sorted into necessary and contingent categories.

Analytic Truth: Traditionally, a statement whose predicate is contained in its subject; a tautology or necessary truth. See **Tautology**.

Argument: An arrangement of statements in which one or more (premises or assumptions) are presented as evidence or support for the truth of another (the conclusion).

Association: A key classificatory operation of the mind, connecting words, ideas, or experiences based on similarity, proximity in time or place, habit, and so on. According the Hume, our idea of causation is rooted in our habitual association of contiguous events. According to Freud, our psyche is revealed in our patterns of word association.

Behaviorism: The theory that mental phenomena, states, and processes can be reduced to, or explained in terms of, observable behavior and/or dispositions to behave.

Belief: An experiential expectation, usually based on mental processing of experiences that have already occurred or are occurring.

Bifurcate: To radically divide, as Descartes divided mind and body, Plato divided ideas and appearances, and transcendentalists divide the divine and the mundane.

Blick: A distinctive way of taking things, a picture of, or perspective on reality. More basic (and less considered than a *weltanschauung*), a blick is rather like a paradigm.

Boolean Algebra: Two-valued logic where the operators are based on negation and the logical AND or the logical OR.

Ceteris Paribus: All things held equal.

Circumstantial: Accidental, contingent.

Common Sense: Whatever beliefs are held by consensus in a community but usually focused on beliefs that are directly supported by everyday experience.

Complement: Every set (or term naming a set) has its complement, which (unlike an opposite) is whatever is not included in the set itself. Thus, the sum of any set and its complement is *everything*.

Connotation: See **Sense**.

Consensus: Common agreement, considerably more than majority opinion but not necessarily unanimous.

Contingent: Circumstantial or accidental, depending on external factors.

Covering Law: A scientific (descriptive) law of very general scope and application and of great explanatory power, thought to be universally true. Covering laws may subsume many particular laws of narrower scope under their aegis, entailing this one or that one in various specific natural circumstances. Example: *Universal gravitation.* See **Hypothesis, Theory,** and **Law**.

Cultural Relativism: The view that value (moral cultural relativism) and/or truth (epistemic cultural relativism) are local to a culture, being produced by the culture itself rather than found in the external world.

Deduction: Argument (or reasoning) is called *deductive* when its grounds offer ironclad support for its conclusion; that is, if it is said to give "closure." Traditionally, the paradigm for deduction was Euclidian proof, typified by inference from general truths to particular outcomes (cf. **Induction**).

Definition:

Essential: Defining a term or phrase in terms of the "essence" of its referents, that is, the universal necessary and sufficient conditions of its use.

Family Resemblance: Defining a term or phrase in terms of overlapping similarities that may be observed in its referents.

Operational: Defining an abstract term or phrase in terms of observable phenomena or operations; for example, defining *gravity* as the acceleration of objects toward one another.

Ostensive: Defining a term or phrase by pointing to its referent.

Paradigm Case: Defining a term or phrase by reference to a stipulated model.

Denotation: See **Reference**.

Dialectic: A process for discovering first principles through probing the presuppositions of common sense beliefs, usually carried out in a question-and-answer dialogue. *Socratic dialectic* aims at debunking false opinions. *Platonic dialectic* seeks underlying reality. *Hegelian dialectic* is the alleged historical process of mind through thesis and antithesis toward synthesis. *Marxian dialectic* sees this historical process as material and economic, not mental.

Distribution: To say that a proposition "distributes" its subject term is say that it makes a claim about each and every member of class named by that term. A term is "undistributed" in a proposition (or "fails to distribute") when the proposition does not make so inclusive a claim. Thus, for example, the proposition "All Athenians are Greeks" distributes "Athenians" (that is, it says something about each and every Athenian) but does not distribute "Greeks" (that is, it does not say something about each and every Greek).

Empiricism: The view that experience (sometimes limited to sense experience) is the primary (or even the exclusive) source of human knowledge (cf. **Modern Rational Empiricism**).

Enlightenment: An age of humanism, naturalism (and some deism), broadly associated with the 18th century.

Epistemic Relativism: The view that the knowable and known vary independently of what is the case, as a function of one's culture, paradigm, mind set, or circumstances; a variety of collective subjectivism.

Epistemology: Knowledge theory, one of the main traditional branches of philosophy.

Evidence: That which is offered as a basis for inferences. It may amount to observations, recollections, axioms of one sort or another, or even revelations. Some kinds evidence are much more reliable than others.

Experience: A covering term for the source of any external data for thought. Usually, sense experience (seeing, tasting, smelling, feeling, hearing), but other input can be included (encounters, visions, and the like). Experience can be objective or subjective, private or public, one-off or replicable.

Experiments: Organized work to test hypotheses, discover new facts, establish connections, and so on. Often done in a lab or in the field and, sometimes (as in the case of *thought experiments*), done in one's head.

Explanation: The rendering intelligible of a state of affairs by carefully noting how it came about and how it relates to other states of affairs (causal), why or for what purpose it occurred (teleological), or the use that it serves (functional).

Extension: Contrasts with **Intension**. See **Reference** and **Sense**.

Felicity Conditions: The circumstances in which a locution is "happy," (for example, a description is felicitous if it is true, a promise is felicitous if it is sincere, a joke is felicitous if it is funny).

Foundationalism: The view that only some states of affairs are directly known and that all other knowledge is derived from that foundation. Different schools of thought pick different foundations.

Hypothesis: A descriptive proposition, not known to be true, that is entertained provisionally in an attempt to explain observed phenomena. It may be narrow or broad in scope and, ideally, will be open to testing in terms of whether or not its various implications are confirmed experientially. Example: *That acquired characteristics can be passed on to one's offspring.* See **Theory, Law,** and **Covering Law**.

Idealism: The metaphysical view that there is a non-physical reality "behind" or "above" the apparent reality of everyday events.

Imply, Entail: To provide sufficient grounds for the truth of, as a premise implies a conclusion. If an implication is logically necessary, it is called an entailment.

Incommensurable: Of two or more statements, theories, or paradigms, not measurable or assessable on a common standard.

Induction: Argument (or reasoning) is called *inductive* when its grounds offer probable support for its conclusion but do not give "closure." Traditionally, the paradigm for induction was generalization, typified by inference from particular truths to universal outcomes (cf. **Deduction**).

Inference: That process of thought by which we move from some grounds or evidence to a thought or opinion said to be based on it or to follow from it. People infer; statements imply. (See **Deduction** and **Induction**.)

In principle: By definition, not accidental.

Intension: See **Sense**.

Intuition: Direct (unmediated) understanding, knowledge, or insight; also unexplained understanding, knowledge, or insight. Often, to say something is intuited is only to say we don't know how we got it.

Invention: Creation. People invent devices, such as telescopes. They also invent ideas, such as the general theory of relativity. Sometimes, invention involves only the synthesis of preexisting bits. Occasionally, however, it involves a *de novo* "leap."

Knowledge: Justified true belief, at least, but more than that according to skeptics who deny its occurrence.

Law: A law is either a prescriptive statement that is desired to be exceptionless (prescriptive law), or a descriptive statement that is thought to be exceptionless (descriptive law). Prescriptive laws (whether common laws or statute laws) are in the realm of social control and are aimed at influencing and directing things in one way or another. Descriptive laws are in the realm of explanation and are aimed at accurately capturing things the way they are. Prescriptive laws may be good or bad, and can be revised when the interests of the law maker change. Descriptive laws may be true or false, and are open to revision in the light of new data. Descriptive laws have *no* prescriptive force. In science, the term 'law' is descriptive and is commonly used as an honorific for a theory that has repeatedly passed rigorous tests across a range of applications. Example: *That for every action, there is an equal and opposite reaction.* See **Hypothesis, Theory,** and **Covering Law**.

Logic: A system of rules of inference to determine whether or not (and, if so, to what extent) the premises of an argument support its conclusion. A rational reconstruction of effective thinking. (See also **Modal, Predicate,** and **Sentential Logic**; also **Boolean Algebra**.)

Logical Empiricism: A philosophical position identified with the Vienna Circle that insisted that all cognitively meaningful language is, in principle, either empirically or formally verifiable; logical positivism.

Logical Form: The syntactical structure of an argument, such as *modus ponens* (that is, "If P, then Q; P, therefore Q") and *modus tollens* (that is, "If P, then Q; Not-P, therefore Not-Q).

Logical Positivism: See **Logical Empiricism**.

Meaning: The sense or the reference (or both) of a word, phrase, or other representation or the intention of one who uses such.

Meaning, Theory of: An account, such as the use theory or the naming theory, of how a word, phrase, or other representation conveys a sense and picks out a reference.

Memory: Recollection or recall or the mental faculty by means of which we recollect or recall. Accurate memory presupposes that what is remembered actually happened the way it is remembered to happen. Not all memory is accurate.

Metaphysics: In Aristotle's collected works, what comes after *Physics*. To logical positivists, nonsense. To the ambitious, speculative "theories of everything." More generally, abstract inquiry about "the furniture of the world." Ontology.

Methexis: Interaction or, in the case of Plato's Forms and the appearances, "participation." Usually occurs in the locution *methexis problem*, as in: "We have no idea how the Cartesian minds and bodies interact. His dualism causes a real *methexis problem*."

Modal Logic: Logic applied to the notions of possibility and necessity (in contrast to the ordinary logic of contingent statements).

Modern Rational Empiricism: The typical epistemological stance of Western science: reason and experience working together to discover, understand, and anticipate facts.

Moral Relativism: The view that what is good, moral, or right varies independently of what is factually the case, as a function of one's culture, paradigm, mind set, or circumstances; a variety of collective subjectivism.

Naming Theory of Meaning: A still common view that words and phrases mean by naming something. It encounters difficulty with such words as *nothing* and such phrases as *the present king of France* (which are meaningful but don't name anything),

Natural Law: "Natural law" may be used as a synonym for "scientific law," in which case the label denotes a strictly descriptive proposition. In many contexts, however, "natural law" is taken to denote one or another *prescriptive* principle of nature. In the latter sense, it has everything to do with religion and metaphysics and nothing to do with science. See **Law**.

Nominalism and Realism: Metaphysical positions on the status of abstract nouns. Realism insists that they name actual entities (such as the Good), while nominalism allows that they express only notions.

Ockham's Razor: The primary tool of theoretical economy; hypothesizing no more than is necessary to save the appearances.

Operationalism: Metaphysical position that abstract nouns must be given operational definitions (see **Definition**).

Opposite: see **Complement**.

Paradigm: Generally, a model, template, or pattern. In recent usage, the frame of reference or perspective in which one operates that determines how things appear and, hence, how one describes or explains them.

Pattern Discernment: Picking out (usually visually but other sense modes can be used) some similarity, structure, organization, or recurrence in occurring experiences; for example, noticing that most of the native residents of Spanish Wells have reddish hair.

Pattern Recognition: Connecting a discerned pattern to a remembered one.

Positivism: The philosophical position of Auguste Comte, typified by the rejection of myth, magic, and metaphysics and the affirmation of "positive science." A precursor of logical positivism.

Post Hoc Ergo Propter Hoc: "After, therefore because of"—a common fallacy.

Postmodernism: A point of view that rejects "modern" rationalism and empiricism, usually focused on Descartes. It is notably committed to both epistemic and normative cultural relativism, trades heavily on such notions as the "sociology of knowledge" and "paradigm shifts," and suggests that *everything* is a text open to interpretation.

Predicate Logic: Logic that involves the analysis of the internal structure of subject/predicate sentences (in contrast to sentential logic, which treats simple sentences as unanalyzed units). The logic of syllogisms and of set theory.

Premise: An assumption or starting point for argument; the basis from which an argument's conclusion is inferred.

Rationalism: The view that genuine knowledge (perhaps all of it) must be achieved through the exercise of the mind rather than through experience (cf. **Modern Rational Empiricism**).

Realism: See **Nominalism and Realism**.

Reason: (1) Cognitive processing, including deductive and inductive inference, classification, hypothesis construction, and the like. Not to be confused with affective processing (the emotions) or conative processing (the will). (2) The basis or grounds for a belief or act. (3) The goal of an act.

Reductionism: A philosophical enterprise that consists of translating accounts of one sort of phenomena into the vocabulary of an allegedly simpler and more inclusive sort of phenomena. Behaviorism, for example, is a reductionist theory of mind.

Reference: Denotation or extension; that which is referred to or picked out by the sense of a word or phrase.

Scholasticism: High medieval thought.

Semantic: Having to do with the sense and reference of language, as opposed to its internal structure or logic. See **Syntactic**.

Sense: The connotation or intension of a word or phrase; the set of characteristics or properties so invoked in terms of which one can pick out the reference.

Sentence, Compound: A sentence composed of two or more simple sentences, joined together (such as "It's 5 o'clock, and I'm ready to quit for the day" and "If I quit now, then I will be home before sundown.") Some compound sentences are truth functions of their components (such as the examples just given), but others are not (such as "John believes that Mary loves Bill").

Sentence, Simple: A sentence no part of which is a sentence in its own right (such as "Today is Friday" and "Grass is green"). See **Sentence, Compound**.

Sentence, Truth-Functional: A compound sentence, the truth or falsity of which is a function of the truth or falsity of its component parts and the meaning of the connector with which those parts are joined. Simple sentences joined by verbal connectors, such as "and," "or," and "if…then," produce truth-functional compound sentences.

Sentential Logic: Logic that examines the implications of simple and truth-functional compound sentences but does not involve the analysis of the internal structure of the simple sentences themselves (as is the case with **Predicate Logic**).

Sociology of Knowledge: The idea, sometimes associated with Karl Mannheim, that what is known is always a function of the culture in which one operates. *Epistemic cultural relativism* is the more common label now.

Sound: The quality of an argument that is valid and has true premises.

State Description: In Newtonian physics, the precise specification of the location and vector of all the bits in a closed physical system. A map of a reality slice.

Syllogism: An argument in predicate logic composed of two premises and a conclusion, each of which has exactly two terms (subject and predicate), each of which occurs twice (one in the first premise and the conclusion, one in both premises, and one in the second premise and the conclusion). See **Predicate Logic**.

Syntactic: Having to do with the internal structure or logic of language (as opposed to its meaning). See **Semantic**.

Synthetic: The character of a statement that cannot be shown to be true or false by logical analysis alone. See **Analytic**.

Theory: A hypothesis that has been well confirmed and, generally, is of sufficiently broad scope to have wide application and utility. Example: *That the physical characteristics of biological organisms are, for the most part, genetically determined.* See **Hypothesis, Law,** and **Covering Law**.

Thinking: The contemplation of an idea, the holding of a belief, or (most notably) using your mind to get from A to B.

Tautology: A statement that is necessarily true, true by virtue of its form, or analytically true (for example, "In base-10 arithmetic, $2 + 2 = 4$," and "If P, then if Q then P").

Truth Conditions: Circumstances in which a statement will be true or false. These may be experiential or logical, at least.

Truth Criteria (Tests): Ideas about how we can ascertain whether a statement is true or not, such as *correspondence* (seeing if it "matches" the way things really are), *coherence* (seeing if it is consistent with other statements that are held to be true), and *pragmatic* (seeing if it works in use).

Truth Theories: Ideas about what makes a statement true, such as *correspondence* (actually matching the ways things are), *coherence* (meshing with other statements that are true themselves), and *pragmatic* (being reliable in use).

Use Theory of Meaning: The theory, associated with Wittgenstein, that the meaning of a statement amounts to nothing more than the uses to which the statement can be put.

Valid: The quality of an argument with a logical form such that the truth of its premises assures the truth of its conclusion.

Venn Diagrams: Graphics used to represent sets, set membership, and the relations between sets by means of overlapping circles, shading, and the placement of Xs. They are used to evaluate syllogisms.

Verification: Testing a statement for truth.

Verificationism: The notion, associated with logical empiricism, that a statement can be meaningful only if it is testable by either experience or logic.

Biographical Notes

The information included here has been gathered from a variety of reference sources, both conventional and electronic. The purpose of these sketches is to identify some of the more influential philosophers and works referred to in the lectures, not to argue their merits. Further information can be found in: *The Directory of American Scholars* (U.S. and Canada), *The Dictionary of National Biography* (Britain), *The Encyclopedia of Philosophy*, and at Web sites such as:

http://www.biography.com/
    Biography.com
http://www.philosophypages.com/
    Philosophy Pages from Garth Kemerling
http://www.newadvent.org/cathen/
    The Catholic Encyclopedia
http://www.utm.edu/research/iep/
    The Internet Encyclopedia of Philosophy
http://www-groups.dcs.st-and.ac.uk/~history/index.html
    History of Math Archive
http://www.formalontology.it/history_of_logic.htm
    History of Logic Bibliography

Aristotle (384–322 BCE). Aristotle was a native of Stagirus in northern Greece. Son of a physician, it is likely that he received some training in that direction himself before his father's death. Later a student (and then a teacher) in Plato's Academy, and eventually founder of his own school (The Lyceum), Aristotle brought a keen interest in methodical observation to philosophy. He was also committed to the notion that all areas of knowledge, especially what we would call the theoretical sciences, can be axiomatised into deductive systems. He was not the first to suggest such a program, however. Indeed, Plato had suggested that there might be a single axiom system to embrace all knowledge; and, at a somewhat more concrete level, Euclid and his axiomatic geometry had come before him. In *Prior Analytics*, he proposed the now familiar syllogistic, a form of logic that, along with the rest of the Aristotelian corpus, became dominant in western thought until the end of the 17th century.

Aquinas, St. Thomas (1225–1274). An Italian Dominican Scholastic theologian, logician and philosopher, Aquinas was markedly Aristotelian in temperament and method. Something of a mystic, and concerned with witchcraft and alchemy, he is most noted by modern philosophers for his monumental works: *Summa Contra Gentiles* and *Summa Theologica*. The definitive voice of Roman Catholic theology and philosophy, Thomas is never an easy read but always a profitable one.

Averroës (1126–1198). Averroës was a notable Arabic philosopher and astronomer whose career came toward the end of the Moorish domination of Spain. He was a major contributor to the preservation of Aristotle's influence on Jewish, Muslim and Christian thought in the Middle Ages.

Ayer, Sir Alfred Jules (1910–1989). An English philosopher, Ayer studied at Oxford under Gilbert Ryle, and (after the war) taught there, at University College London, and again at Oxford as Wykeham Professor of Logic from 1959. His most influential book was *Language, Truth and Logic*, a forceful introduction of Logical Empiricism to the English-speaking world. Other works include *The Problem of Knowledge* and *The Central Questions of Philosophy*. Your lecturer was privileged to attend his lectures at Oxford in 1975, and found him as witty and astute at the lectern as he was at his writing desk.

Bacon, Sir Francis (1561-1626). The son of Nicolas Bacon, the Lord Keeper of the Seal of Elisabeth I, Francis Bacon entered Trinity College, Cambridge, at age 12. He turned to the law and at 23 he was in the House of Commons. He rose to become Lord Chancellor of England, and fell in the course of a struggle between King and Parliament. Rejecting Aristotelianism and Scholasticism, Bacon saw himself as the inventor of a new method, *Novum Organum* (1260), which would kindle a "a light that would eventually disclose and bring into sight all that is most hidden and secret in the universe." His method involved the collection of data, their judicious interpretation, the carrying out of experiments, thus to learn the secrets of nature by organized observation of its regularities. Bacon's proposals had a powerful influence on the development of science in seventeenth century Europe. Thomas Hobbes served as Bacon's last secretary.

Boole, George (1815-1864). Son a a shoemaker (with interests in scientific instruments that distracted him from his cobbling) and a lady's maid, Boole began his education at a tradesmen's school. With a passion for languages, he became proficient in Latin, Greek, German and French without formal training. Boole began correspondence with De Morgan in 1842 and wrote a paper applying algebraic methods to differential equations that was published in 1844. In November 1849 Boole became the first Professor of Mathematics at Queen's College, Cork, where he taught the rest of his life. In 1854 he published *An investigation into the Laws of Thought, on Which are founded the Mathematical Theories of Logic and Probabilities*. This began the development of "Boolean algebra," now an important component of the "languages" of computers and switching circuits.

Comte, Auguste (1798–1857). A French thinker, the inventor of sociology and the founder of classical positivism, Comte argued that science has emerged from theological and metaphysical stages into its modern "positive" (operational or experiential) posture, and that human reverence should be for humanity itself. His works include six volumes on *Positive Philosophy* and four on *Positive Polity*. He is said to have practiced what he called "mental hygiene" by avoiding reading the works of others.

Copernicus, Nicholaus (1473–1543). The son of a Polish copper trader and educated at the University of Krakow, Copernicus studied Latin, mathematics, astronomy, geography and philosophy. Astronomy then consisted of mathematics courses which introduced Aristotle's and Ptolemy 's view of the universe so that students could understand the calendar, calculate the dates of holy days, and navigate at sea. While a student, Copernicus also became familiar with Euclid's *Elements*, the Alfonsine Tables (planetary theory and eclipses) and spherical astronomy. Notable as the author of what we now call the "Copernican Revolution," he brought three tools of thinking to the table: painstaking observation, mathematical/logical skill and the creative capacity to reconceptualize what we observe under a new paradigm.

DeMorgan, Augustus (1806-1871). Born in India, DeMorgan was educated at Trinity College, Cambridge, where he matriculated at the age of 16 in 1823. He began the use of a slash to represent fractions, perfected the principle of Mathematical Induction (1838), and made many contributions to the development of symbolic logic, including "DeMorgan's laws." He held the chair in mathematics at University College, London, from which he resigned (twice) on issues of principle. Not a warm person, he is remembered for his devotion to abstract reasoning.

Descartes, René (1596–1650). A French rationalist philosopher and mathematician, Descartes was Jesuit trained and strictly Catholic, but no Scholastic. He was notable for his reconstruction of rational knowledge by way of systematic doubt. Apart from the "cogito" and everything built on it, he is also noted for the invention of analytic geometry. His notable works include *Discourse on Method* and *Meditations on First Philosophy*. The model Cartesian tool of thinking is precise deduction. The bases of that deduction are to be found in those indubitable truths that are available to us (such as, allegedly, the axioms of geometry). If such "necessary" truths are not available, of course, there will be issues about the output of our thinking, however fool-proof the tool we use to process our data.

Einstein, Albert (1879–1955). Born in Germany, Einstein had a lackluster record in his early schooling there. He continued his education at the Zurich Technical High School, and after becoming a Swiss citizen in 1901found temporary employment as a secondary shool mathematics and physics teacher in Winterthur. While employed at the Bern Patent Office (1902–1905), Einstein wrote numerous artcles on topics in theoretical physics in his spare time and completed a Ph.D. at Zurich in 1905. In the years that followed, Einstein contributed to his own "Scientific Revolution" by way of his Special and General theories of relativity and his reconceptualization of space and time. He also contributed to the philosophical revolution from genetic to confirmational empiricism. Not only at the forefront of all things theoretical (though he did not share the general enthusiasm for Quantum Mechanics), he was also influential in international affairs. Eventually a citizen of both Switzerland and the United States, he was an unflagging advocate of world peace.

Euclid of Alexandria (circa 325 BC–circa 265 BC). Euclid is best known for his treatise *The Elements*. Little is known of his life except that he taught at Alexandria. There is even argument about whether he actually existed. Most likely, he was a student of Plato and lived during the reign of Ptolemy I. Whether the content of *The*

Elements is wholly (or even in part) his own, that work set the pattern for "axiomitizing" bodies of knowledge. We are also in Euclid's debt for the pattern of *"reductio ad absurdum"* proof (where we assume the falsehood of an hypothesis and, by showing that this leads to absurdity, infer that the hypothesis is true).

Frege, Gottlob (1848-1925). Son of a schoolmaster in Wismar, Frege entered the University of Jena shortly after the Seven Years' War, and completed his doctorate at Gottingen in 1873. He returned permanently to Jena in 1874 where he taught all branches of math; but his works on the philosophy of logic, mathematics and language are key. In 1879 his *Begriffsschrift*, a book on "conceptual notation," laid out a logical system with negation, implication, universal quantification, and the essential idea of truth tables. His *Foundations of Arithmetic* (1884) attempted to axiomatize it, in keeping with his belief that it is reducible to logic. In 1902, Frege received a letter from Bertrand Russell pointing out a contradiction in his system of axioms. This generated lengthy correspondence and a revision to an axiom, but the system remained inconsistent.

Galileo (1564–1642). Born near Pisa, the son of a musician and teacher, Galileo seemed destined for a careeer in medicine but was seduced by mathematics. An early reader of Euclid and Archimedes, he abandoned his medical studies altogether by 1585. A student of the theory of motion, he worked out many important ideas (such as the parabolic path of a projectile), but they were not published until the 1630s. In 1609 he came into possession of a spyglass, took up lens making, made telescopes, and turn his gaze skyward. This serendipitous combination of intellect and artifact (creative thinking and a telescope) opened the door to a thorough reconceptualization of the universe and our place in it.

Heisenberg, Werner (1901–1976). Born in Würzburg, Germany and educated at the University of Munich, Heisenberg is remembered for his contributions to physics in the form of matrix mechanics, quantum mechanics, atomic structure and the indeterminancy principle. Calling Newtonian notions about causation and predictability in question, he contributed heavily to the twentieth century "revolution" in theoretical physics. While there may be no questions about accuracy of quantum mechanics, there are questions about its implications. Heisenberg's own interpretations of them, in *Physics and Philosophy* (1962), are controversial.

Hume, David (1711–1776). A Scottish philosopher and historian, Hume studied at Edinburgh, but was denied professorships there and at Glasgow for religious reasons. His many important works include *An Inquiry Concerning Human Understanding, A Treatise of Human Nature,* and *Essays Moral and Political.* He was the definitive British Empiricist, noted for his views on causation, the association of ideas and the roots of induction in habit rather than in demonstrable truth. He is notably credited for awakening Kant from his "dogmatic slumbers" and for his aversion to "sophistry and illusion." His long-term influence on British Analytic philosophy is unmistakable at every turn, but is especially evident in the works of Russell, Ryle, Wittgenstein, Austin and your present lecturer.

Kant, Immanuel. (1724–1804). A German philosopher, perhaps the first *professional* philosopher, Kant was a career academic. His three *Critiques* (of *Pure Reason, Practical Reason* and *Judgment*) are landmarks in modern philosophical history, responding to Hume's empiricism and permanently marking out the limits of reason in such as way as to exclude any knowledge whatever of "things in themselves." Most of the subsequent philosophical discussion of the analytic/synthetic distinction and of the impossibility of synthetic *a priori* knowledge has been influenced for good or ill by his notions of the "transcendental analytic."

Kepler, Johannes (1571-1630). Son of a mercenary soldier who died in war, Kepler began life in Swabia and was raised by his mother in her father's inn. After school and a regional seminary, he enrolled at the University of Tübingen. Now remembered for the laws of planetary motion named for him, he also worked with optics and made discoveries in solid geometry, demonstrated how logarithms work, and contributed to the eventual development of calculus. Not only a keen mathematician, he was also a painstaking observer. His remarkably precise astronomical tables also helped to establish the truth of heliocentric astronomy.

Kuhn, Thomas (1922–1996). An American philosopher and historian of science, Kuhn taught at Harvard, Berkeley, Princeton and MIT. His *The Structure of Scientific Revolution* was published at mid century as a volume in the *International Encyclopedia of Unified Science*—a surprisingly positivistic venue for a non-positivistic treatise. If Kuhn did not invent paradigms and paradigm shifts, he certainly put them on the map for the rest of us. On his view, there is no rational basis for choosing one paradigm over another. Other works include *The Essential Tension: Selected Studies in Scientific Tradition and Change* and *The Road Since Structure: Philosophical Essays, 1970-1993*.

Mill, John Stuart (1806–1873). Born in London, the son of the Scottish philosopher James Mill, and the product of an early excursion into home schooling, Mill took on Greek at the age of 3, Latin and arithmetic at 8 and logic at 12. With the security of a nominal career at the India Office, he devoted much time to the Utilitarian Society, the Westminster Review, and the London Debating Society. His first major work, *A System of Logic*, was published in 1843. Later important pieces include *Liberty* (1859), *Utilitarianism* (1863) and *Three Essays on Religion* (1874). His influence on Bertrand Russell and John Maynard Keynes was substantial. The reputation of Mill's *Logic* was largely due to his analysis of inductive proof. He sought to provide the empirical sciences with a set of formulas and criteria which might serve the same purpose for them that the formulas of the syllogism had served for classical deductions from general principles.

Newton, Sir Isaac (1643–1727). The most famous of English scientists, Newton entered Trinity, Cambridge, to prepare for law in 1661 (after a thoroughly spotty career in school). The slightly non-restrictive atmosphere there allowed him to read widely (including Aristotle, Descartes, Gassendi, Hobbes, Boyle, Galileo and Kepler). He started reading mathematics in 1663, by way of a book on Astrology, but soon progressed to Euclid and to the analytical geometry and algebra of Descartes and Viète. When the plague closed the University in the summer of 1665 Newton returned to Lincolnshire where, in two years time, he began revolutionary advances in optics, physics, and astronomy, and laid the foundations for differential and integral calculus, several years before its independent discovery by Leibniz. Best remembered for the laws of motion constituting "Newtonian Mechanics," he laid out the basic dimensions of orthodox scientific thinking for the next two centuries, before turning his attentions away from science and mathematics for the last half of his life.

Peano, Giuseppe (1858–1932). Son of a farming family in the Piedmont, Peano began his education at a village school but completed it at the University of Turin. He went on to teach there in

1880. In 1887, he published a method for solving systems of linear differential equations, and in 1888, a geometrical calculus including a chapter on mathematical logic. In 1900 he presented at the International Congress of Philosophy in Paris. Of him, Bertrand Russell said, in his *Autobiography*, "this was the turning point of my intellectual life ... In discussions at the Congress I observed that [Peano] was always more precise than anyone else, and that he invariably got the better of any argument on which he embarked. ... I decided that this must be owing to his mathematical logic ... an instrument of logical analysis such as I had been seeking for years."

Peirce, Charles Saunders (1839–1914). A man of notably erratic temperament and son of a Harvard astronomer/mathematician, Peirce was born in Cambridge and educated at Harvard himself. Early research with the U.S. Coastal Survey into geodesy and gravimetrics, and his work on Boolean logic, led to contact with such logicians as W. S. Jevons and Augustus De Morgan. Noted for his essays "The Fixation of Belief" and "How to Make our Ideas Clear," Peirce was appointed to a position at Johns Hopkins in 1879 where he developed a theory of relatives and quantifiers independently of Frege's work. His career was beset with difficulties in the wake of his indiscretions; but his influence (particularly by way of Pragmatism, of which he was a primary founder) was substantial in the long run.

Plato (427–347 BCE). Student of Socrates, founder of the Athenian Academy, and teacher of Aristotle, Plato exercised the dialectical method not only to discover error but also to lead the way to insight. While we may debate the accuracy of the details of his insights, the broad sweep of the Platonic message remains intriguing. Plato's notions of the human mind, will and appetites, his fundamental models for social organization, and his basic dualism of appearance and reality, have all found their way (through Aristotle, Descartes and others) into the modern mind set. Of primary interest here is his notion that the mind (in pre-existent circumstances) once had immediate access to reality (the Forms), and that the process of thought that leads to present understanding is essentially one of elucidating (through dialectic) what the mind remembers of what it already knows.

Popper, Karl (1902–1994). A very influential Austrian philosopher of science and politics, Popper insisted in *The Logic of Scientific*

Discovery (1935) that scientific knowledge never advances by proving the truth of a theory (since that is impossible), but only through the systematic experiential falsification of alternatives to one. His controversy with Wittgenstein is legendary. In the long run, his political philosophy (in *The Open Society and Its Enemies*), has had greater impact than his theory of falsification; but that theory certainly influenced the development of Logical Empiricism, being particularly prominent in A. J. Ayer's accounts of that movement.

Port Royal Logic (1662). Port Royal was a Jansenist convent near Paris, noted by logicians for *The Port Royal Logic*, one of the most widely used philosophical works of the 17th century. This volume dealt with traditional logic with a strong Cartesian flavor, and was in the vernacular. Written by Antoine Arnauld (1612–1694), and Pierre Nicole (1623–1695), and first published anonymously, it was translated into many languages and was widely influential.

Quine, W. V. O. (1908–2000). Son of an engineer and a school teacher, Quine was educated at Oberlin and Harvard. Having read James's *Pragmatism* in school, and Russell and Whitehead's *Principia Mathematica* as an undergraduate (!), he turned to mathematics and philosophy of mathematics at Harvard where, after his PhD, he was appointed Junior Fellow in 1933 and instructor in philosophy in 1936. The lines of influence between Quine, the Logical Positivists, Russell and Whitehead were many and mutual. A prolific writer, perhaps his most influential essay was "Two Dogmas of Empiricism" in which he called empirical orthodoxy into serious (pragmatic) question, arguing that "it is folly to seek a boundary between synthetic statements, which hold contingently on experience, and analytic statements, which hold come what may." Your lecturer had the honor to meet him at Oxford in 1974, finding him terse and more than a little intimidating, but warmly interested in the work of a young philosopher from the provinces.

Russell, Lord Bertrand (1872–1970). An English philosopher, logician, mathematician, freethinker and essayist, Russell was a student, fellow and professor at Cambridge, where he influenced the shape of philosophy for generations (by way of "both" Wittgensteins as well as the Vienna Circle), and set the course of all subsequent philosophy of logic and mathematics. His early works included *Principles of Mathematics* and *Principia Mathematica*. Mid-career books included *An Enquiry into Meaning and Truth* and *Human*

Knowledge, plus myriad essays and polemics on topics ranging from education and marriage to nuclear disarmament. Social and political issues were his primary focus after 1949.

Socrates (470–399 BCE). A legendary, not to say mythic, figure in Western intellectual history, Socrates is remembered as the teacher of Plato, the gadfly of Athens, an alleged corrupter of youth and worshipper of false gods, and the master of what has come to be called "Socratic dialectic." Convinced that wisdom begins in the realization of ignorance, Socrates committed himself to convincing one and all—in maddening conversations—of just how ignorant we are. Since Socrates appears repeatedly as a major player in the Platonic dialogues, it is not at all easy to know where Socrates leaves off and Plato takes over. It is likely, however, that the dialectical method of inquiry itself is truly Socratic. The notion of dialectic has been corrupted historically in the metaphysical schemes of Hegel and Marx.

Venn, John (1834-1923). Grandson of the founder of the Clapham Sect (a socially progressive religious movement) and son of the Secretary of the evangelical Church Missionary Society for Africa and the East, Venn was educated at Gonville and Caius College, Cambridge. Ordained a priest himself, Venn eventually pursued an academic life, with strong interests in both literature and mathematics. He significantly extended Boole's mathematical logic and is remembered for his diagrammatic representations of sets and their relationships with three circle figures. The relationships of these circles nicely represent the structure of all 256 types of classical categorical syllogisms.

William of Ockham (c.1280–c.1349). An English Scholastic, Franciscan and philosophical nominalist, Ockham studied theology at Oxford (perhaps under Duns Scotus) and Paris, where he taught. Charged with heresy, and subsequently a refugee in Bavaria, he denied papal authority over temporal matters. A dogged opponent of metaphysical *largess*, he is more remembered today for his "razor" than for any particular treatise.

Wittgenstein, Ludwig (1889–1951). A Viennese/English philosopher, inventor and sometime schoolteacher, Wittgenstein studied engineering at Berlin and Manchester and mathematical logic at Cambridge, where he taught (with lengthy interruptions) between 1929 and 1947. The most influential Western philosopher of the 20th century, Wittgenstein's two major works, *Tractatus Logico-Philosophicus* and *Philosophical Investigations,* laid the foundations for Logical Atomism and Logical Positivism, on the one hand and for "ordinary language analysis" on the other. Neither an easy person nor an easy philosopher, this brilliant and quirky thinker stirs interest even among non philosophers, as evidenced by the reception of David Edmonds' and John Eidinow's *Wittgenstein's Poker.*

Bibliography

Essential Reading:

Asimov, Isaac. *Asimov's Chronology of Science and Discovery.* New York: Harper Resource, 1991, ISBN 0062700367. Asimov's work is notable for its combination of scientific accuracy and accessibility to the general reader. This particular book will give you a good overview of the sweep of scientific progress and, more important, an insight into the methodology by which that progress was won.

Copi, Irving. *Introduction to Logic.* 11th ed. Upper Saddle River, NJ: Prentice-Hall, 2002, ISBN 0130337358. This book is clear and meticulous and covers all the bases, from informal logic (critical thinking), through classical and modern treatments of the syllogism and the basics of symbolic deductive logic, to inductive reasoning and probability. It has many useful exercises and has gone through many editions. The 11th, cited here, is not the latest, but it is readily (and cheaply) available on the used-book market.

Hempel, Carl. *Philosophy of Science.* Upper Saddle River, NJ: Prentice Hall, 1966, ISBN 0136638236. Not the newest but one of the best presentations of "mainstream" 20th-century philosophy of science. The book is short, clear, thorough, and uncompromising. Hempel's posture is empirical, as far as evidence is concerned, but his empiricism is nuanced in terms of the issues laid out in the next citation. Most important for present purposes, Hempel lays out a clear analysis of how hypotheses work in scientific explanations and of how they are formulated and supported.

Kuhn, Thomas S. *The Structure of Scientific Revolutions.* 3rd ed. Chicago: University of Chicago Press, 1996, ISBN 0226458083. This is where all the talk of "paradigms" and "paradigm shifts" comes from. As usual, you should have a look at the source of these notions before you make up your mind about the popularizers use (and misuse) of them. Kuhn is trying to show that science is not inevitably progressive and that its movement over time is not linear. Another important idea that crops up here is that scientific claims are "theory laden" and, hence, *not* "value-free." If so, then the tools that scientists use in their thinking are influenced by the immediate scientific milieu and by the larger culture in essentially political ways. This book channels Wittgenstein into postmodernism. It is not easy going.

Recommended Reading:

Aristotle. *Prior Analytics*. Robin Smith, ed. Indianapolis: Hackett Publishing, 1989, ISBN 0872200647. Here, as with other volumes mentioned below, we are indebted to Hackett for a high-quality edition of a classical text at an affordable price. This part of Aristotle's legacy is devoted to basic logic. It is the wellspring of the enterprise in the west.

Ayer, A. J. *Language, Truth and Logic*. New York: Dover Publications, 1952, ISBN 0486200108. This is the classic manifesto of logical positivism in English. Ayer's skeptical rejection of everything "metaphysical" fairly bristles. It is not for the fainthearted. Even though this sort of aggressive empirical reductionism was reined in by Wittgenstein's move to "ordinary language," this is still a good account of the knowledge/evidence connection.

Beck, Lewis White. "Constructions and Inferred Entities." *Philosophy of Science*, XVII, 1950. Reprinted in *Readings in Philosophy of Science*, Herbert Feigl and May Brodbeck, eds. New York: Appleton-Century-Crofts, 1953. This essay explores the status of the unobservable "bits" that modern science has so much to say about, showing how scientific theory is empirical even though it is not directly about what we see, taste, smell, feel, and hear. It is a classic presentation of the essential role of responsible hypothesis construction in science.

Berlinski, David. *Newton's Gift: How Sir Isaac Newton Unlocked the System of the World*. New York: Free Press, ISBN 0743217764. This work captures the scope and impact of Newton's "revolution" with just enough attention to the technical side to make it useful for non-scientists in getting a handle on the history of science. It also provides useful insights into Newton himself and his era. The style is a little arch but not unbearably so.

Best, Joel. *Damned Lies and Statistics*. Berkeley: University of California Press, 2001, ISBN 0520219783. Evidence is important, but some evidence is much more important than the rest. Written strictly for the popular market, this book is about the difference. It will either teach you how to mislead others with statistics or how to avoid letting them mislead you. It is transparent, important, and funny and should be universally required reading.

Butler, Christopher. *Postmodernism—A Very Short Introduction.* Oxford: Oxford University Press, 2002, ISBN 0192802399. Part of an excellent new series, this (very) little book will help the reader figure out what is going on when people start talking about *deconstruction* and other things "postmodern." Much has been said in recent years to suggest that modern philosophy and modern science are hopelessly flawed and that all "knowledge" is local, relative, and agenda- and culture-driven. A few hours with this book will help the reader see the grounds and implications of those allegations and make a judgment about their merit.

De Kruif, Paul. *Microbe Hunters.* New York: Harvest Books (Harcourt), 2002, ISBN 0156027771. This is the original "gee-whiz" book about the heroes of modern medical discovery. Every boy and girl should read it for inspiration. Every adult should read it for increased understanding and appreciation of how hands-on experimental inquiry is done. Medical and scientific progress is not easy or cheap.

Descartes, René. *Meditations.* Indianapolis: Hackett Publishing, 1999, ISBN 0872204200. Rationalism embodied. It has been said that all of modern philosophy amounts to either the embellishment or the repudiation of Descartes. This little book is the nub of the matter. Here, "systematic doubt" allegedly leads to the deductive reconstruction of all knowledge from one necessary truth (*cogito ergo sum*). Empiricists disagree.

Dewey, John. *The Quest for Certainty.* Carbondale, IL: Southern Illinois University Press, 1988, ISBN 0809314932. Too often overlooked (perhaps because of its turgid style), this is a very important presentation of why epistemologies such as Descartes' rationalism are doomed by their improper inclusion of "certainty" as one of the necessary conditions of knowledge. Dewey's own pragmatic reconstruction of knowledge makes it provisional, dynamic, and possible (in contrast to Descartes', which leaves it absolute, static, and unobtainable).

Fearnside, W. Ward. *Fallacy: The Counterfeit of Argument.* Upper Saddle River, NJ: Prentice-Hall, 1959, ISBN 0133017702. Not new, but worth scouting out on the Web for a used copy, this book catalogs (and gives examples of) just about every informal fallacy there is. Somebody needs to do a 21st-century update with current examples from the media, but the fallacies themselves haven't changed, and this is a handy place to learn what they look like.

Hall, James. *Practically Profound*. Lanham, MD: Rowman & Littlefield, 2005, ISBN 0742543277. Modesty prevents me from assessing the quality of this and the next item. Suffice it to say here that most introductions to philosophy don't take the time to tackle the question of what makes various beliefs and opinions good, bad, or indifferent. This one does.

————. *Logic Problems for Drill and Review*. Washington, DC: University Press of America, 1991, ISBN 0819183792. This little book contains the skeleton of symbolic deductive logic, plus several hundred problems (with solutions). If you want to learn logic from scratch, I recommend Copi. But if you want a quick profile (or a review), this will be useful.

Hawking, Stephen W. *The Illustrated Theory of Everything: The Origin and Fate of the Universe*. Los Angeles: New Millennium Press, 2003, ISBN 1932407073. This book is not cited because it is *true* or even because your lecturer *thinks* that it is true. It is cited because it dramatically illustrates the sweep of mature modern rational empiricism. No one should either dismiss science (whether on postmodern, religious, or other grounds) or pay homage to it without reading this book (alongside Asimov's *Chronology*, cited above).

Hempel, Carl. "Problems and Changes in the Empiricist Criterion of Meaning." *Revue Internationale de Philosophie*, Vol. 1, No. 11, 1950. Reprinted in *Classics in Analytic Philosophy*, Robert R. Ammerman, ed. Indianapolis: Hackett Publishing, 1990, ISBN 0872201015. This is the classic account of the core of logical positivism's "verificationism." It shows the pitfalls in this brand of rational empiricism and sketches out possible ways to work around them. The book in which this is reprinted is a gem of a collection. Kudos to Hackett for getting it back in print and keeping it there. When you have read Hempel's essay, read the others.

Huff, Darrell. *How to Lie with Statistics*. New York: W. W. Norton & Co., 1993, ISBN 0393310728. This book is a cousin of Joel Best's little volume, cited above. It is less a handbook for deceiving others than a manual for avoiding statistical landmines yourself. This is an enjoyable (even amusing) read, but more important, it is a crucial guide to how mathematics can be used and misused in "proofs," scientific or otherwise.

Hume, David. *An Enquiry Concerning Human Understanding.* Eric Steinberg, ed. Indianapolis: Hackett Publishing, 1993, ISBN 0872202291. Empiricism embodied. This book does for empiricism what Descartes' *Meditations* did for rationalism (but with greater success). Hume, too, dances with skepticism. As a result, he arrives at a rather startlingly confined profile of what we know. The treatment of induction and causation, the analysis of beliefs in terms of habits of mind, and the dismissal of "sophistry and illusion" are legendary. No serious thinker can ignore this work.

Jones, W. T. *A History of Western Philosophy*, Volume I, "The Classical Mind." Belmont: Wadsworth Publishing, 1969, ISBN 0155383124. The five-volume series is old, but the presentation is balanced and the commentary is illuminating. The advantage and the disadvantage of Jones's approach both lie in his reliance on lengthy quotations from the primary sources. This may tempt the reader to avoid tackling the primary sources head on, but it also helps the reader see whether or not Jones's own analysis is responsible to the texts.

Mill, John Stuart. *A System of Logic: Ratiocinative and Inductive.* New York: Harper and Brothers, 1891. Available as a reprint from University Press of the Pacific, ISBN 1410202526. Far too expensive for a casual purchase, this work can be found in any nearby college library. It is the source of "Mill's method," the backbone of inductive reasoning as it is presented in standard logic texts, such as Copi's (cited above).

Okasha, Samir. *Philosophy of Science—A Very Short Introduction.* Oxford: Oxford University Press, 2002, ISBN 0192802836. Short, excellent, and current, if not as systematic and meticulous as Hempel's treatment (cited above). This book will give the reader an idea of what the current issues are among those who try to map and explain what scientists are up to.

Pinker, Steven. *How the Mind Works.* New York: W.W. Norton and Company, 1997, ISBN 0393318486. If there are any tools of thinking, surely the mind is one of them. But the mind has been the subject of more heat than light in philosophical discussions over the last 2,000 years. Pinker brings neuroscience and other modern tools to the analysis of how this tool operates. This is an exciting read and is totally accessible to the layman.

Plato. *Meno.* G. M. A. Grube, trans. Indianapolis: Hackett Publishing, 1980, ISBN 0915144247. Plato's ideas about how the mind works are not like Pinker's. This little dialogue lays out his basic notion that "recollection" is the key to learning, thinking, and understanding. But that presupposes the preexistence of the "soul" and the objective reality of the "Forms." This is the taproot of traditional rationalism and mind/body dualism.

————. *Republic.* G. M. A. Grube, trans. Indianapolis: Hackett Publishing, 1974, ISBN 0915144094. This is Plato's gem. Everyone should read it for its political, social, and moral implications (some of which are chilling, as noted by Karl Popper in his masterpiece, *The Open Society and its Enemies*—a book worth chasing down). What is of interest here, however, is Plato's conceptions of appearance and reality, the mind (cognitive soul), and knowledge. In the Myth of the Cave, Plato lays all that out metaphorically. The point is the same as in the *Meno*, and if the metaphor is supposed to describe reality, then the metaphysical price tags (and their Cartesian legacy) are even more obvious.

Popper, Karl. *The Logic of Scientific Discovery.* New ed. New York: Routledge, 2002, ISBN 0415278449. In this work, Popper disputed one of the initial tenets of logical positivism, viz. that all meaningful propositions are verifiable in principle. Because that would rule out universal claims, however, Popper suggests that all meaningful propositions are falsifiable in principle. This is all explained nicely in Hempel's essay, cited above. The value of this book is not to be found in the details of the arguments over verification and falsification, however. Its value resides in the notion that scientific discovery is hypothesis driven. This, too, is explained well in the Hempel essay, as he discusses scientific *method.*

Quine, W. V. O. "Two Dogmas of Empiricism." In *From a Logical Point of View.* Cambridge: Harvard University Press, 1980, ISBN 0674323513. Reprinted in *Classics in Analytic Philosophy.* Robert R. Ammerman, ed. Indianapolis: Hackett Publishing, 1990, ISBN 0872201015. This essay calls into question the notion that there is a bright-line distinction between analytic and synthetic statements (and, derivatively, between *a priori* and *a posteriori* knowledge). If there is no such bright-line distinction, then the traditional distinctions between deductive and inductive reasoning need to be rethought. This article contributed in a major way to the postmodern relativizing and pragmatizing of secure inference.

Rosenberg, Jay F. *The Practice of Philosophy: Handbook for Beginners.* 3rd ed. Upper Saddle River, NJ: Prentice Hall, 1995, ISBN 0132308487. This simple book lays out basic philosophical methods in very attractive and intelligible form. Reading it will help you understand what is going on in the philosophical essays and books that you read.

Schilpp, P. A. *Albert Einstein: Philosopher-Scientist.* Chicago: Open Court Publishing, 1988, ISBN 0875482864. We are indebted to Professor Schilpp for a large set of volumes about 20th-century philosophers, of which this is one. Here you will find Einstein's statement of his own philosophical/scientific outlook, numerous essays by his contemporary critics, and his reply to them. It is not a scientifically technical collection. It is about the broad sweep of Einstein's thought.

Turing, A. M. "Computing Machinery and Intelligence." *Mind*, Vol. LIX, No. 236 (1950). Reprinted in *Minds and Machines*. Allen Ross Anderson, ed. Upper Saddle River, NJ: Prentice Hall, 1964. This really is a classic. The point of bringing it up is that it was one of the first persuasive essays written that suggested the *possibility* of artificial intelligence. This has become very important as the computer has become more and more central as a thinking tool.

Unger, Peter. *Ignorance, A Case for Skepticism.* Oxford: Oxford University Press, 2002, ISBN 0198244177. This is a definitive presentation of modern radical skepticism. You don't have to agree with Unger to see the power of his arguments to the effect that no one ever knows anything. Of course, if he is correct, then it doesn't matter whether you agree with him or not. Your lecturer does not agree with Unger, and I have tried to refute the line of argument he takes in my *Practically Profound*. I bring him up here simply because everything we have explored about *how* we know presupposes the possibility of knowing something—a presumption that we cannot ignore.

White, Jamie. *Crimes Against Logic.* New York: McGraw-Hill, 2004, ISBN 0071446435. This is another treatment of fallacious reasoning. It is less systematic but far more amusing, than Fearnside's work, cited above.

Internet Resources

Critical thinking:

http://www.austhink.org/critical/
http://www.criticalthinking.org/

History of logic:

http://www.formalontology.it/history_of_logic.htm

History of mathematics:

http://www.maths.tcd.ie/pub/HistMath/

History of science:

http://www.fordham.edu/halsall/science/sciencesbook.html

History of science emphasizing chemistry (Chemsoc timeline):

http://www.chemsoc.org/timeline/index.html

History of ideas and inventions:

http://www.ideafinder.com/history/index.html
http://inventors.about.com/

History of calculators and computers:

http://www.xnumber.com/xnumber/ (click on "vintage calculators")
http://www.hitmill.com/computers/computerhx1.html